Mr. Tiger

Al Kaline: 1934-2020

THE LEGEND OF AL KALINE, DETROIT'S OWN

Detroit Free Press

The lineup

E **Editor**
Gene Myers

D **Designer**
Ryan Ford

CE **Copy editor**
Jennifer Troyer

PE **Photo editing**
Ryan Ford

PI **Photo imaging**
Tanya Ramirez

SE **Free Press sports editor**
Chris Thomas

ST **Special thanks**
Noah Amstadter
Peter Bhatia
Owen Davis
Anne Delay
Bill Dow
Kevin Heard
Megan Holt
Kathy Kieliszewski
Beth Myers
Dora Robles Hernandez
Andrew P. Scott
Bill Smith
Brooke Thomas
Angie Walton
Eros & Schrodinger

Photo credits
COVERS: MALCOLM EMMONS
PAGE 1: MALCOLM EMMONS
PAGE 3: ALAN R. KAMUDA

MANDI WRIGHT

Across the street from Comerica Park, the Fox Theatre paid tribute to Hall of Famer Al Kaline, who died April 6, 2020. Tigers owner Chris Ilitch, CEO of his family's sports, entertainment and pizza empire, said "baseball lost a titan."

Detroit Free Press

COPYRIGHT © 2020 BY THE DETROIT FREE PRESS

No part of this publication may be reproduced, stored in a retrieval system or transmitted in any form by any means, electronic, mechanical, photocopying or otherwise, without prior written permission of the publisher, Triumph Books LLC, 814 North Franklin Street; Chicago, Illinois 60610.

ISBN: 978-1-62937-859-6

TRIUMPH
BOOKS

TRIUMPHBOOKS.COM
@TriumphBooks
⬡ Triumph Books LLC
⬡ 814 North Franklin Street, Chicago, Illinois 60610
⬡ Phone: (312) 337-0747

Mr. Tiger

THE LEGEND OF AL KALINE, DETROIT'S OWN

Al Mighty

When Al Kaline made his Tigers debut in June 1953, he was a mere boy of 18. Nearly seven decades later, he was a Detroit icon — the face of the franchise, hailed as much for his gentility and humility off the field as he was for his greatness on it.

With Tiger Stadium as the backdrop, Al Kaline posed for a portrait in the 1960s. His Hall of Fame career spanned 22 seasons, from June 1953 to October 1974. Note the lack of batting gloves on his hands and protective earflaps on his helmet.
MALCOLM EMMONS

Al Kaline's 22 years, 2,834 games and 3,007 hits were just the start of a lifelong love story with Detroit

A Tiger for all seasons

BY JOHN LOWE

Al Kaline, who in a long and unique Detroit Tigers lifetime grew from youthful batting champion to Hall of Famer to distinguished elder statesman, died April 6, 2020, at his home in Bloomfield Hills, Michigan. He was 85.

Kaline's health had been declining over the past year. Neither the family nor the team revealed a cause of death. However, general manager Al Avila said it was not related to the novel coronavirus pandemic.

"One of the most distinguished and decorated players in the history of baseball, Mr. Tiger was one of the greatest to ever wear the old English D," the Tigers said in a statement. "The Hall of Famer has been a pillar of our organization for 67 years."

Kaline was survived by his wife of 65 years, Louise; sons Mark and Michael; four grandchildren; and one great-grandchild.

CONTINUED ON PAGE 10

In April 2000, during a charity gala for the Atanas Ilitch Osteosarcoma Foundation, Al Kaline basked in the glow of the first public lighting of new Comerica Park and the unveiling of the statues of five Tigers Hall of Famers. Kaline was almost speechless when he saw his statue for the first time. "It's great," he said of the figure reaching high to make a catch.
J. KYLE KEENER

Mr. Tiger's quick hits

FULL NAME: Albert William Kaline.

NICKNAME: Mr. Tiger.

BORN: Dec. 19, 1934, in Baltimore.

HEIGHT: 6-feet-1.

WEIGHT: 175 pounds.

BATS: Right.

THROWS: Right.

FAMILY: Wife, Louise; sons Mark and Michael.

HALL OF FAME: Inducted in 1980. Elected in first year of eligibility with 88.3% of the vote.

DETROIT TIGERS: Outfielder/first baseman/designated hitter, 1953-74; TV broadcaster, 1976-2001; special advisor to owner Mike Ilitch, 2001; special assistant to president Dave Dombrowski, 2002-15; special assistant to general manager Al Avila, 2015-20.

CAREER HIGHLIGHTS: Batted .297 with 399 homers, 3,007 hits, 1,582 RBIs in 2,834 games. ... Won 10 Gold Gloves as an outfielder (1957-59, '61-67). ... Won AL batting title in 1955 with a .340 average — at 20, youngest batting champion. ... Hit .379 (11-for-29) with two homers and eight RBIs in 1968 World Series. ... Became 12th player to record 3,000 hits. ... Selected to 18 All-Star Games. ... Posted a .324/.375/.514 slash line — 12-for-37 with two homers, six RBIs, seven runs. ... Won Roberto Clemente Award (1973), Hutch Award (1969), Lou Gehrig Award (1968). ... Was first Tiger to have number (6) retired (1980). ... Was AL's seventh-youngest player at 18 in his first season (1953) and fifth-oldest player at 39 in his last season (1974).

Al Kaline famously turned down the first $100,000 salary offer in Tigers history between the 1970 and 1971 seasons. He signed for $96,000, same as his 1970 contract, in part because he didn't think his statistics had been up to par. General manager Jim Campbell, to generate off-season publicity, decided to throw in an extra $4,000 after the fact. "I told Jim, 'No, we have a contract.' ... I couldn't take it," Kaline said in 2010's "Al Kaline: The Biography of a Tigers Icon" by Jim Hawkins. Near Christmas in 1971, Kaline finally signed for six digits.
DETROIT FREE PRESS

Pandemic delayed ceremony

For a decade, thousands of Michiganders bid farewell to a series of sporting giants in public visitations at large venues. Because of the novel coronavirus pandemic, that wasn't possible when Al Kaline died in April 2020.

In 2010, Tigers broadcaster Ernie Harwell lied in repose at Comerica Park. In 2016, Red Wings legend Gordie Howe lied at Joe Louis Arena. In 2017, Tigers and Wings owner Mike Ilitch lied at the Fox Theatre. In 2019, Wings Hall of Famer Ted Lindsay lied at Little Caesars Arena.

Tigers general manager Al Avila said the week of Kaline's death that Mr. Tiger would be laid to rest in a private ceremony. Avila also said that at some point the Tigers would hold a public ceremony — likely at Comerica Park.

Kaline died during Gov. Gretchen Whitmer's stay-at-home executive order for Michigan and the Centers for Disease Control and Prevention's guidelines of no public gathering of more than 10 people.

Avila promised that Kaline would be "honored the way that a man of his stature should be."

— Anthony Fenech

Al Kaline tossed out the ceremonial first pitch during the 1984 World Series, flanked by commissioner Peter Ueberroth (left), in his first month on the job after spearheading the Los Angeles Olympics, and civil rights icon Benjamin Hooks, executive director of the NAACP at the time.

MARY SCHROEDER

CONTINUED FROM PAGE 6

In 22 seasons with the Tigers, most of them as a marvelous rightfielder, Kaline played in more games and hit more homers than anyone else in club history, and he compiled a batting resume second only to Ty Cobb's.

But while Cobb was widely reviled for his bitterness and meanness, Kaline was widely and eminently respected for his on-field elegance and off-field graciousness.

Thus, Kaline has a strong claim as the most distinguished Tiger of them all.

Albert William Kaline was born in a working-poor section of Baltimore on Dec. 19, 1934. His father was a broom maker. His mother scrubbed floors. When Kaline received a reported $35,000 signing bonus from the Tigers in 1953, he paid off the mortgage on his parents' home and paid for an eye operation for his mother.

"They'd always helped me," he said. "They knew I wanted to be a major-leaguer, and they did everything they could to give me time for baseball. I never had to take a paper route or work in a drugstore or anything.

"I just played ball."

Kaline signed with the Tigers the morning after he graduated from high school — and made his major-league debut a week later. He would never play in the minors. He would never wear any uniform but Detroit's.

Hall of Fame glove and bat

Kaline was 39 when he played his final game in 1974. Days before his career ended, he had reached one of baseball's most cherished milestones when he recorded his 3,000th hit. But he finished with 399 home runs, and on the final day of his career he left the season-ending game with several innings remaining and thus lost a few at-bats in which he could have bid for the 400th homer.

But statistics never captured how special Kaline was. Like the Yankees' Joe DiMaggio and the Cardinals' Stan Musial, he embodied the beauty of the game and became a living monument of how gracefully it could be

CONTINUED ON PAGE 13

Although usually referred to as "Mr. Tiger" for more than half a century, Al Kaline's nickname with his Tigers teammates and many Detroit fans during his playing days was simply "Six."
DETROIT FREE PRESS

In July 2018 at Cooperstown, Al Kaline welcomed Tigers right-hander Jack Morris (left) and shortstop Alan Trammell to baseball's most exclusive club. "He was very proud," Trammell said, "that some more Tigers were joining him in the hall."
ERIC SEALS

CONTINUED FROM PAGE 10
played.

Hall of Fame voters didn't seem bothered that Kaline didn't hit 400 homers. In his first year of eligibility, he was elected with 88% of the vote by baseball writers — well above the 75% required for induction.

Yet the humble Kaline said he was "shocked" when he learned he had been elected. After the Hall of Fame's initial class in 1936, only nine others before Kaline were elected in their first year on the ballot, a list of diamond luminaries that included Musial, Ted Williams, Willie Mays, Mickey Mantle and Jackie Robinson but not DiMaggio, Cy Young, Hank Greenberg or Yogi Berra.

Kaline is one of the few dozen players in baseball history to get 3,000 hits. Like his contemporary, Pittsburgh rightfielder Roberto Clemente, Kaline is a member of the 3,000-hit club who is remembered nearly as much for his defense as for his offense — perhaps just as much. In one game as a rookie, Kaline threw out a Chicago White Sox runner for three consecutive innings — at home, third and second. The Sporting News said of a robbery he made in 1956 at Yankee Stadium: "No one who saw it will forget how Kaline shot above the rightfield scoreboard in the stadium to make a great one-handed catch on Mickey Mantle."

Kaline is one of six Tigers with a statue behind the left-center fence at Comerica Park. And despite his 3,007 hits and those club-record 399 homers, that statue shows him not with a bat in hand, but making a leaping, one-handed catch like the one he

CONTINUED ON PAGE 15

On the day of Al Kaline's death in April 2020, lifelong Tigers fan Kyle Ziolkowski, a 30-year-old Detroiter, visited Comerica Park for a photo of Kaline's statue.
MANDI WRIGHT

JULIAN H. GONZALEZ

Al Kaline, in a scene repeated countless times over the decades, chatted with a young ballplayer during spring training in Lakeland, Florida. This 2014 visit was with Jose Iglesias, a 24-year-old shortstop from Cuba.

CONTINUED FROM PAGE 13

made on Mantle.

Yet without his superb defensive skills, Kaline likely would have made the Hall of Fame on his hitting alone. Every eligible player who has gotten 3,000 hits has entered the hall except for Rafael Palmeiro, whose candidacy was short-circuited by a positive test for steroids soon after his milestone base hit in 2005. Kaline won the American League batting title as a 20-year-old in 1955, and although he never won another batting title, he never stopped hitting.

In Kaline's final season, ace Baltimore pitcher Jim Palmer said of him: "I like to watch him hit. I like to watch him hit even against us. He's got good rhythm, a picture swing. Other hitters could learn a lot just by watching him. The thing about Kaline is that he'll not only hit your mistakes; he'll hit your good pitches, too."

Palmer recalled how in his first big-league start, in 1965, he struck out Kaline looking on three pitches the first time they faced each other. The second time up, Palmer said, he threw Kaline a fastball, curve and change-up. Kaline hit the change-up for a two-run homer.

After one year out of baseball following his retirement, Kaline joined the Tigers' television team in 1976 as the analyst for play-by-play man George Kell, a former Tigers third baseman. Kell, also a Hall of Famer, and Kaline, after a rough learning curve, provided engaging, incisive commentary on Tigers telecasts for the next two decades. When Kell retired from broadcasting, Kaline

CONTINUED ON PAGE 16

CONTINUED FROM PAGE 15

worked on the air with play-by-play men Ernie Harwell and then Frank Beckmann into 2001.

Before the 2002 season, new club president Dave Dombrowski appointed Kaline as a special assistant. He was a frequent inhabitant of the field and clubhouse throughout his 70s and 80s. After owner Mike Ilitch fired Dombrowski during the 2015 season, Kaline remained in the front office as a special assistant for Avila.

Short on a homer, long on humility

By never playing in the minors and wearing a Tigers uniform for every game, Kaline is in a very small group of players who performed for one team and one team only throughout his pro career. Another was a Hall of Fame contemporary, left-handed pitcher Sandy Koufax of the Dodgers. They faced each other twice, in All-Star Games in 1960s, with Kaline singling and fouling out.

Baseball's rules of the 1950s kept Kaline and Koufax out of the minors at the start of their careers. Back then, there wasn't an amateur draft — the vehicle that gives one club exclusive signing rights to an amateur player. To keep down the bidding wars on amateur players in those predraft days, the rules mandated that any player signed for more than $4,000 would have to spend two years in the majors before he could be sent to the minors for seasoning.

The Tigers thought Kaline was well worth that possible inconvenience. When he came out of high school in Baltimore in 1953, the Tigers spread the word they had signed him for $35,000, a figure repeated countless times over the decades. However, in interviews for a 2010 book, "Al Kaline: A Biography of a Tigers Icon," Kaline told author Jim Hawkins: "It was a $15,000 bonus, plus two years' salary of $6,000 each, which was the major-league minimum at the time."

Still, for a bonus worth $140,000

ALAN R. KAMUDA

In August 1980, the Tigers retired Al Kaline's No. 6 — a first in their 79-year history. Hall of Fame second baseman Charlie Gehringer showed off the jersey to the big crowd. Gehringer coached Kaline in the 1951 Hearst Sandlot Classic at New York's Polo Grounds, an all-star game for prep stars across the country run by Hearst newspapers. With an inside-the-park homer, a single and several outstanding catches, Kaline, 16, was voted the game's MVP. "He was so small I didn't see how he'd ever make an outfielder," Gehringer said, "and I tried to get him to play second base." In 1983, in a dual ceremony, Gehringer's No. 2 and Hank Greenberg's No. 5 were the next numbers retired by the Tigers.

in today's dollars, Kaline essentially went straight from high school graduation to the Tigers. He was 18 years and six months old when he played his first game for Detroit on June 25, 1953.

By the time Kaline was eligible to go to the minors in 1955, he was on the way to that season's batting title.

He was 20 years old when he finished that season with a .340 average, 21 points higher than anyone else in the league and 12 days younger than Cobb was when he won the 1907 title. At 20 years and 280 days, Kaline remains the youngest batting champion in American League history.

CONTINUED ON PAGE 20

In the third inning at Tiger Stadium, Willie Horton greeted Al Kaline after he touched 'em all for the second time off Minnesota's Jim Kaat on June 22, 1967. At 32, Kaline was off to one of his best starts: .329, 15 homers and 51 RBIs in 64 games. But another injury — this one self-inflicted — awaited five days later. Upset after striking out against Sudden Sam McDowell, Kaline broke a finger slamming his bat into the rack. He missed a month. His final numbers were very good — .308, 25 homers, 78 RBIs in 131 games — but who knows what might have been. The Tigers lost the pennant to Boston on the season's final day.
LES POOSCH

Who was the baby-faced ballplayer? In the winters early in his career, before moving full-time to Detroit, Al Kaline worked in a sporting goods store in Baltimore. That helped him follow advice that Ted Williams gave him in 1953: swing a heavier bat a half-hour a day and squeeze a baseball all the time during the off-season.
DETROIT FREE PRESS

In a 1999 column, Ernie Harwell wrote of Al Kaline: "The consummate pro for 22 seasons. A brilliant fielder and clutch hitter. Too bad this great team player appeared in only one World Series."

'Best kid player I ever scouted'

In the 1990s and 2000s, legendary Tigers broadcaster Ernie Harwell wrote a weekly column and four books for the Detroit Free Press. For May 29, 1998, he wrote about Al Kaline's high school scouting report.

As I was rummaging through old papers, I found an article I had written about Al Kaline for The Sporting News on Jan. 20, 1962.

Al was 27 years old and about to enter his 10th season as a Tiger. My story focused on the Tigers' scouting report of Al when he was a 15-year-old high schooler in Baltimore. Scout Ed Katalinas provided me with that original assessment of the future Hall of Famer.

The 1950 report said this about Kaline:

1. Showed outstanding arm.

2. Has good speed.

3. Excellent body control.

4. Natural outfielder (CF).

5. Best kid player I ever scouted.

6. Have four years to watch develop.

One of Kaline's neighbors gave Katalinas the first tip on Kaline. ... Ed scouted Kaline for four years and signed him to a Tigers contract in 1953, the day after he graduated from Southern High School.

JIMMY TAFOYA

There wasn't a Take Our Daughters and Sons to Work Day in the 1960s — it's the fourth Thursday in April these days — but the Tigers' daddies could bring their boys to the ballpark. Sons Mark and Mike were with Al Kaline in 1965.

CONTINUED FROM PAGE 16

After that, Kaline's highest finish in a batting race was second, which he achieved three times. He also twice placed third in the late 1960s. He never led the league in homers or runs batted in, and he never won its most valuable player award (he twice finished second and once third in the MVP voting).

But Kaline hit .300 or better in nine seasons, and he finished with a .297 lifetime average. In 10 seasons he won a Gold Glove as one of the three best defensive outfielders in the American League. In his later years, he played often at first base as well as in the outfield. In his final season, he served exclusively in a role that the AL had instituted the year before — designated hitter.

Kaline won the respect of the Boston outfielder who is widely regarded as the greatest hitter in history. This became evident one day as Kaline sat in the media dining room at Fenway

Park before doing the telecast of a Tigers-Red Sox game. Into the room swooped Ted Williams. He knew his entrance would require him to fend off the Boston press with which he had long feuded. But he had an important mission, as he growled at the reporters who approached him. "I just came in here to say hello to Al Kaline," he said.

Boston wasn't filled with such kindness for Kaline in 1967. In that season, he was selected as an All-Star for the 13th straight year. But in the same season, he had a right to wonder whether he would be among the handful of all-time great players who never reached the World Series.

For the first several years of his career, Kaline and the rest of the American League basically were blocked from the World Series by a New York Yankees dynasty. Not only were those the days before the draft caused talent to be more equally

CONTINUED ON PAGE 22

Family's final request: Check on loved ones

Despite all the thousands and thousands of glowing words written about Al Kaline after his death, his family still paid for an eight-paragraph obituary in the Detroit Free Press.

It appeared on a Sunday, to reach the largest audience, six days after his passing, tucked on the sixth of nine pages of death notices.

It included a nod to Tigers fans: "Al was always grateful for the love and support fans in the city and the state showed him over the years, as well as all the Tigers and Major League Baseball provided for him and his family."

It included typical Kaline humility: "Al felt that the game, the team and the city gave him far more than he gave in return."

It ended with a special request: "In lieu of flowers or donations, the Kaline family asks that you reach out to someone you love and check in on them during this unprecedented and challenging time of need, and to be sure to thank our military, police, fire/EMS and frontline caregivers in any way you can."

– Kirkland Crawford

Al and Louise Kaline posed with sons Mark, 11, and Mike, 6, in the summer of 1968. Joe Falls wrote in the Free Press: "Al Kaline lives on a quiet, tree-shaded lane in the picturesque village of Franklin. Just down the road is an old wooden cider mill. ... Kaline lives in an air-conditioned ranch house. ... 'Nobody has to tell me how much I have,' said Kaline as he sat out on his patio with a frosted ice tea at his side."
DICK TRIPP

The milestones

FIRST GAME: June 25, 1953, at Philadelphia Athletics; replaced Jim Delsing in centerfield in the sixth inning of a night game.

HITTING: Became the 12th player to reach 3,000-hit plateau. Second to Ty Cobb in Tigers history with 3,007. Became youngest batting champion with a .340 average in 1955, 12 days younger when Cobb won the title in 1907.

HOME RUNS: Total of 399 is the Tigers record. Nine times hit 20 or more homers.

DURABILITY: Tied Tris Speaker's American League record by playing at least 100 games for 19 consecutive seasons (1954-72).

FIELDING: Won 10 Gold Gloves as an outfielder. Set AL record by playing 242 consecutive games in the outfield without an error between May 15, 1970 and July 2, 1972.

BEST GAME: Walked, then collected four straight hits, including three home runs, versus Kansas City Athletics on April 17, 1955. Two home runs and eight total bases in the sixth inning of that game tied major-league records.

3,000TH HIT: Sept. 24, 1974, a double in his hometown of Baltimore off Dave McNally. First Tiger to reach 3,000 hits since Cobb. First American League to reach 3,000 since Eddie Collins in 1925.

ALL-STAR GAMES: Made the AL team 18 times, seven as a starter and 13 consecutive years (1955-67). Played in 16 games, missing two because of injuries. Had 12 hits in 37 at-bats for a .324 average, with two homers, six RBIs, seven runs, two walks, one double, one steal, one hit-by-pitch and six strikeouts. Finished with a .324/.375/.514 slash line. Never made an error in an All-Star Game.

CONTINUED FROM PAGE 20

distributed, but also they were the days before the major leagues were split into divisions. There were thus no playoffs within the leagues; the teams that finished first in the American and National leagues advanced directly into the World Series.

In Kaline's first 12 seasons, the Yankees won 10 pennants. Then the Yankees' dynasty abruptly collapsed, and a few years later, in 1967, the Tigers made their first down-to-the-wire run at the pennant in Kaline's career. They were eliminated when they lost their final game of the season. Boston — not Detroit — won its first pennant since the mid-1940s.

But the next year, 1968, the Tigers were not to be stopped, and they didn't even need a huge season from Kaline. The team had a narrow first-place lead in the AL in late May when Kaline suffered a broken forearm. When he returned

CONTINUED ON PAGE 23

CONTINUED FROM PAGE 22

five weeks later, the Tigers were well on their way to the pennant. They won it by 12 games with a 103-59 record. The MVP of the Tigers and the AL was right-hander Denny McLain, who became the first (and still only) pitcher to win 30 games in a season since the 1930s.

Typical of Kaline's humility, he questioned whether he even deserved to be in the starting lineup for the World Series. He said he didn't see how manager Mayo Smith could bench Mickey Stanley or Jim Northrup, who had gotten most of Kaline's at-bats when he was injured. After his return July 1, they kept playing and Kaline logged only 191 at-bats. For the season, he started and finished only 58 games in rightfield. According to a Joe Falls exclusive in the Free Press the day after the pennant clincher, an emotional Kaline said, "I don't deserve to play in the World Series."

CONTINUED ON PAGE 24

JUNFU HAN

In September 2018, with the Cardinals in town, the Tigers held a 50th reunion of the 1968 World Series champions. Old warriors (left to right) Willie Horton, Mickey Stanley and Al Kaline threw out ceremonial first pitches. The Tigers won that night, 5-4, like the '68 Tigers — in walk-off fashion.

CONTINUED FROM PAGE 23

But with four outfielders for three starting spots, Smith came up with a daring solution for the World Series against St. Louis: He moved Stanley from centerfield to shortstop to replace light-hitting Ray Oyler, even though Stanley had played only nine games there in the big leagues. Kaline returned to rightfield for the World Series, and he batted .379 with eight RBIs. His 11 hits in the Series included two homers, two doubles and perhaps the biggest hit of the Series and of his career.

The Tigers were within a few innings of elimination when Kaline batted with the bases loaded and one out in the seventh inning of Game 5 at Tiger Stadium. He delivered a two-run single that turned a one-run deficit into a one-run lead. The Tigers never trailed again in the Series. They won Game 5, then went to St. Louis and beat the Cardinals in Games 6 and 7. At 33, Kaline had played on his first and only pennant winner and world champion.

In the following season, 1969, baseball expanded and went to divisional play. In 1972, Kaline played on a first-place finisher for the second and final time. Kaline, at age 37, got into one of the hottest hitting stretches of his career in the final days of the season and helped the Tigers edge Boston by a half-game for the East Division title. Over his last 10 games, eight of which the Tigers won, Kaline batted .512 (21-for-41) with four homers, eight RBIs and 15 runs scored.

If the Tigers had beaten Oakland in the playoffs, Kaline would have been back in the World Series. But in the winner-take-all final game of the playoff series, Oakland snuck out of Tiger Stadium with a 2-1 victory. The potential tying run in the decisive Game 5 reached first base in the seventh, eighth and ninth innings against Vida Blue: Aurelio Rodriguez made the third out in the seventh, Kaline made the second out and

CONTINUED ON PAGE 25

CONTINUED FROM PAGE 24

Duke Sims the third out in the eighth, and Tony Taylor made the game's final out.

Kaline's 3,000th hit represented a major circle closing. It came in his hometown of Baltimore on Sept. 24, 1974. He had 2,999 hits when the game began. He grounded out in his first at-bat. In his second, he hit an opposite-field double down the rightfield line off left-hander Dave McNally for No. 3,000. "He hit a fastball that went right across the plate," McNally said. "I got an autographed ball from him that day."

Eight days later, on the final day of his career, Kaline's humility surfaced again and perhaps cost him a chance at his 400th homer. There are a few accepted ways for a star to take his final bow: leave the field for a defensive replacement in the late innings or take a late-game at-bat. Either way, the crowd can give the departing stalwart one last resounding ovation.

Kaline chose neither route in his finale, which was played against Baltimore on a Wednesday afternoon in early October in front of a mere 4,671 at Tiger Stadium. He couldn't take a final trot in from his defensive position because he was the DH, as he was every time he played that season. So his final appearance would come in the batter's box.

Kaline had hits in 13 of his previous 15 games but he hadn't homered since Sept. 18 off Boston's Reggie Cleveland, his 13th of the season.

In his first two times up that day against the Orioles and left-hander Mike Cuellar, Kaline struck out looking and flied to left. His next turn at-bat came with two out and one on in the fifth inning. Instead, he allowed manager Ralph Houk to send up Ben Oglivie to hit for him against right-hander Wayne Garland.

The small gathering of fans was thus denied the chance to salute Kaline and to see him take a few more at-bats in pursuit of the 400th homer. According to one report, "the crowd booed thunderously."

Afterward, Kaline explained that he had injured his left shoulder over the weekend, realized that he lacked the strength to hit a home run and asked Houk to remove him from the game. "I was sitting there in the clubhouse and I could hear them booing," Kaline said. "I really felt sorry for Ben. It wasn't his fault."

Houk said: "With a hitter as great as he is, you don't send him back out there when he says he's had enough. I think I owed Al that much."

Kaline's early exit was so stunning, the fans' reaction so overwhelming and the media's coverage so negative toward the Tigers that Kaline still faced questions about it on the January 1980 day that he was elected to the Hall of Fame.

"That was one of my most embarrassing moments," Kaline said years later. "But you have to understand that I didn't realize at the time the fans came out to see me in my last time at-bat."

Kaline made his permanent home in the Detroit area from early in his Tigers career. But in his later role as assistant to the president, he often went with the Tigers on their trips to Baltimore. In one such homecoming instance, he showed that he was anything but a frontrunner. He joined the Tigers on their trip to Baltimore early in the 2003 season when they had a 4-25 record and already were being

CONTINUED ON PAGE 27

Al Kaline's first hit at Michigan and Trumbull came Aug. 27, 1953, a single to right in the seventh inning against Washington right-hander Spec Shea in Briggs Stadium. Kaline's last hit came Oct. 1, 1974, a single to center in the eighth inning against Baltimore right-hander Jim Palmer in Tiger Stadium.

MALCOLM EMMONS

In the early days of spring training in February 2003, Al Kaline hit grounders to pitchers during infield practice. Imagine if the 69-year-old Hall of Famer hadn't helped out: The '03 Tigers finished 43-119, one loss fewer than the modern-era futility record held by the 1962 New York Mets.
JULIAN H. GONZALEZ

CONTINUED FROM PAGE 25
called one of the worst teams ever, which it turned out they were.

'The best I ever played against'

When Kaline was eight, he was diagnosed with osteomyelitis and two inches of bone were removed from his left foot. Despite a permanent deformity and constant pain throughout his life — "it's like a toothache in the foot," he once explained — Kaline quickly developed into a skilled athlete in a baseball-playing extended family.

First, Kaline was a pitcher. That made sense, because his father and grandfather were catchers. "My grandfather was a bare-handed catcher in the old Eastern Shore League," Kaline said on his first day in the big leagues in 1953. "And my father was an amateur catcher around Baltimore."

Kaline recalled that when he was 12, he went 10-0 on his neighborhood team. But when he went out for his high school team as a freshman, his coach put him in the outfield because of his strong and accurate arm. "That was the best break I ever got," Kaline said in 1955, the season he became a star.

Major-league scouts descended on Kaline's high school games. The competition for him came down to the Tigers and a few other teams willing to make him "a bonus baby" — the player whose signing bonus was big enough that he had to spend those two years in the majors before he could go to the minors.

Early in his Detroit career, Kaline said, "I signed with the Tigers because they had shown the most interest and because I thought I might get a chance to play oftener with them." In 1952, the Tigers had lost 104 games. In 1953, they lost 94 more. Years later, Kaline admitted he turned down more money from the Philadelphia Phillies and Boston Red Sox to sign with the Tigers.

KALINE FAMILY

Al Kaline, born Dec. 19, 1934, in Baltimore, told the Free Press in 1968: "We lived right behind a power factory. Every time I take my kids to Baltimore ... I show them that power factory and those three smokestacks. I just want them to know that life was never always this easy."

In his first full season, 1954, Kaline took over as the Tigers' rightfielder. By mid-1955, when he became eligible to be sent to the minors, he was starting in the All-Star Game and was on the way to the batting title. Plus, his team finished with a winning record.

"Everything I hit that year fell in or was in the hole," he said a quarter-century later. "That, and the pitchers didn't start pitching me cute until August. In effect they were saying they'd rather take their chances with me and pitch around the big guys. Then they must have decided, 'Hey, this guy's for real.'"

When he broke Hank Greenberg's club record for career homers, Kaline said, "How can anyone compare me with Greenberg? I'm not a home-run hitter." Kaline's single-season high in homers was 29 — exactly half of the club-record 58 that Greenberg had

swatted in 1938.

But consistent excellence is baseball's greatest jewel, and Kaline delivered it for two decades. By 1970, his 17th full Tigers season, he noticed he was getting applause in parks throughout the American League. "This makes a guy feel good," Kaline told The Sporting News. "Most of it is for being around so long. I've stood the test of time. And I haven't done anything to embarrass the game or myself."

The same can be said of Clemente, the Pirates' star and humanitarian who died in a plane crash in the winter of 1972-73 while en route to help earthquake victims in Nicaragua. Like Kaline, Clemente broke in during the mid-1950s, played his whole career with one team and piled up 3,000 hits and innumerable defensive marvels. Upon Clemente's death, Major League Baseball renamed in his honor its annual award for the player who "best exemplifies the game of baseball, sportsmanship, community involvement and the individual's contribution to his team."

In 1973, the first time it was given as the Roberto Clemente Award, the winner was Al Kaline.

While Clemente served in many ways as Kaline's mirror image, Baltimore third baseman Brooks Robinson became his alter ego. Like Kaline, Robinson was a dangerous hitter who was one of the best defensive players ever at his position. And like Kaline, Robinson continually presented a mix of class, competitiveness and humility.

In Kaline's final season as a player, Robinson said: "When you talk about all-around ballplayers, I'd say Kaline is the best I ever played against. And he's a super nice guy, too.

"There aren't too many guys who are good ballplayers and nice guys, too. Your attitude determines how good you're going to be — in life as well as in baseball. He's got a great attitude."

Gene Myers contributed to this report.

2

The cat's meow

6

A superstar? No, that wasn't Al Kaline — at least according to him; he was just a regular guy. Everyone else, though, knew better and had their own story — a hit they couldn't believe, a throw they'd never seen, a kindness that was stunning.

The cheers rained down on Al Kaline on Sept. 27, 1999, before the final game at Tiger Stadium. "I again find myself humbled by this place," he said. Rightfielder Karim Garcia, wearing No. 6 as a tribute, hit the game-winning homer.
JULIAN H. GONZALEZ

Despite 132 more plate appearances on the road than at home, Al Kaline did most of his slugging at Michigan and Trumbull. He hit 226 homers at home and 173 on the road — or a homer every 22.1 at-bats at home compared to a homer every 29.7 at-bats on the road.

MALCOLM EMMONS

Few could match Al Kaline's quality on the field, or his kindness off it

The perfect player

BY MITCH ALBOM

With so much death around, one man's passing can go unnoticed. This one did not. Even with the shroud of coronavirus taking us down in shocking numbers, no one in Michigan was numb to the news that arrived with a gasp April 6, 2020: Al Kaline was gone.

Mr. Tiger takes his bow. At a time of year when baseball should be puffing its lungs, Al Kaline exhaled his last breath at 85.

"I just talked to him over the weekend," his former Tigers teammate and dear friend Jim Price said, fighting tears after hearing the news. "It was difficult. He didn't sound right. I said, 'Al, call me. I'm worried about you.' He said he would. But of course ... he couldn't."

He choked up. "I'm heartbroken."

Aren't we all? Al Kaline, who we all seemed to know, who was always around, who spent nearly seven decades of his life affiliated with the Detroit Tigers, was gone.

But his legend lives.

CONTINUED ON PAGE 32

J. KYLE KEENER

A month before Comerica Park's opening, technician Rory Heberling applied a protective coating to a stainless steel Al Kaline, designed by the Pennsylvania husband-wife sculptors Omri Amrany and Julie Rotblatt-Amrany.

CONTINUED FROM PAGE 31

That verdict is already in. Kaline hasn't played a baseball game since 1974, but he is still one of the first Tigers that come to mind when you say "great ones."

He hasn't been on the air for nearly 20 years, yet his voice — like that of Ernie Harwell — still rings in the ears of Tigers fans everywhere.

"Baseball lost a titan," Tigers owner Chris Ilitch said in a statement.

A titan, yes. But in accomplishment only. Inside his No. 6 uniform, inside his sport coat and open collar, inside a television booth, or a banquet hall, or a charity event, Al Kaline never played a titan. He was simply a man. A good, kind man.

Which is the only way he saw himself.

And why we saw him as so much more.

Mr. Tiger takes his bow.

'Seemed like a good-bye'

"I had dinner with him a few weeks back, during spring training," said Jim Leyland, the former Tigers manager. "We went to the Terrace in Lakeland. We laughed about old times, we talked about old times, we talked about the players, the GMs ...

"After the dinner, we went home to the Residence Inn and we got to the door he gave me a hug. He said, 'Gimme a hug, Jim.' So I gave him a hug. And he said, 'You know, Jim, thanks for being my friend all this time.'

"It was almost like he knew something, he probably wasn't going to see me again. ... I went back to my room and laid there. And I said to myself, 'That almost seemed like a goodbye.'

"And, obviously, it was."

Heartbreaking. Yet if Kaline saw the end coming, so many of us did not. Consumed by the COVID-19 pandemic rattling the globe, we were sideswiped by the news, and left scrambling to put his life into some perspective.

Here is a try.

This was a beaming star who never let the glow get in his eyes, a Baltimore kid born into poverty, the son of a broom maker, who signed his first contract at age 18 the morning after

CONTINUED ON PAGE 34

On Al Kaline Day in August 1970, Al and Louise circled Tiger Stadium to a standing ovation. Sons Mark and Mike rode in the front seat. Kaline's pal Gordie Howe received nearly as loud a reception as the star of the festivities. Booed heartily were commissioner Bowie Kuhn, manager Mayo Smith and Michigan Gov. William Milliken. Also, Cherry Street bordering Tiger Stadium was renamed Al Kaline Drive.
MIKE MCCLURE

"Al Kaline was almost what you'd call the perfect player. Maybe not the perfect talent, but the perfect player."

– Jim Leyland, former Tigers manager

CONTINUED FROM PAGE 32
his high school graduation. A man who won a batting title at age 20, who made 18 All-Star Games, who played until he was 39, who inspired the 1968 Tigers to that classic World Series title, who collected 3,000 hits, who still holds the franchise record for home runs at 399 and who once threw out three baserunners in three straight innings — from rightfield!

This is a man who got hitting tips from Ted Williams, who smacked a hit off Satchel Paige, who once went into an auto parts business with Gordie Howe, and who made the Hall of Fame on his first ballot.

But this is also a man who asked, upon signing his first contract, if he could still play in an amateur game a few days later because he had promised the guys he would do so. A man who once refused a pay raise when he didn't think he'd earned it. A man who was shy and reverent around older, accomplished stars, who was self-conscious about his grammar when broadcasting games, and who never announced himself to a room and would often go unnoticed in it, until some blinking observer with his mouth dropping open would gush, "Hey, isn't that Al Kaline?"

It was. He would offer that bright smile, and a handshake, maybe an old story. And another fan would forever be in awe.

'The perfect player'

"When I got traded here in 1967," Price recalled, "Mickey Stanley and Gates Brown greeted me, and Al walked by and said, 'Who's this kid?' And they said, 'This is our new catcher, Jim Price.' And he said, 'Welcome, kid.'

"He was the leader. He was our future Hall of Famer. We put him on a pedestal. ... We revered him, even at that time. If there were bats to be picked up, we picked them up. If there were extra balls, we'd say, 'Al, you don't pick them up, we will.'

"If we had a fight, we said, 'Al, you stay in the dugout, we'll do the fighting. You stay in the dugout.' Those were the orders."

Still, despite those efforts, Kaline's career was not without pain. As a boy, he had two inches of bone in his left foot removed, and he had to learn to run on the side of his foot. In the majors, he ran into a wall and injured his knee. He once broke a finger slamming his bat into a rack. And he suffered a broken forearm during the 1968 campaign, and actually suggested to manager Mayo Smith that he sit out the World Series because other players had earned it more.

No way that was going to happen. Instead, Smith made the now-famous move of juggling the lineup, moving Stanley to shortstop to get Kaline into rightfield. The Tigers rebounded from a 3-1 deficit to win the championship.

Over the years, Kaline proved himself on offense and defense with equal aplomb. He always had an amazing arm. Legend has it that as a high schooler, during a picnic competition, he threw a ball 173.5 feet in the air (nearly 60 yards). The judges didn't believe it, so they made him try again. This time he threw it 175 feet. It is a story that belongs in Bernard Malamud's "The Natural."

And in many ways, that's who he was.

"He played the game to perfection,"

CONTINUED ON PAGE 35

Despite missing a month with a broken finger, Al Kaline wasn't kneeling down on the job in 1967. In his first down-to-the-wire pennant race, at 32, he finished third in batting (.308) and WAR (7.5), fourth in runs (94) and OPS (.952), and fifth in home runs (25).
MALCOLM EMMONS

CONTINUED FROM PAGE 34

Leyland said. "Al Kaline was almost what you'd call the perfect player. Maybe not the perfect talent, but the perfect player."

The perfect player has left us. But it's not the bat and glove that will define his legacy. After all, it's been years since we saw him play baseball. But so many Michiganders are telling the tale of him shaking their hands, or sharing a story, or encouraging their kids, or laughing at a memory. As Leyland points out, "I call him 'Mr. Gentleman.' Because he was a gentleman who happened to be a great Tiger, not vice versa."

Amen to that. It's not Al Kaline's dying that makes us sigh. It's the life he led, and the fact that we may never see its likes again.

Mr. Tiger takes his final bow. Summer feels a long way off.

Once a frightened rookie, now a kindly icon —
Al Kaline always found a way to brighten your day

A superstar next door

BY JEFF SEIDEL

I walked up to Al Kaline at the National Baseball Hall of Fame in Cooperstown, New York, which was surreal especially since he was standing so close to his plaque.

It was like approaching baseball royalty in the room where they keep the crowns and thrones.

"Mr. Kaline, yesterday, I met a girl here in Cooperstown whose name is Kaline," I said.

It was in 2018 at a reception before Jack Morris and Alan Trammell were inducted into the hall.

"I wrote a story about her," I said.

"I know!" he said. "I met her today and we took a picture."

He paused for a beat.

"Usually, they name dogs after me," Kaline said, smiling. "This is the first girl."

He laughed. That is how I'll remember Kaline — full of humility, humor, grace and elegance.

Next-door neighbor

I don't remember watching Kaline play — I was 7 when he retired from the Tigers in 1974.

ERIC SEALS

Blame (or credit) the Chicago father for naming his daughter after his favorite Tiger. Kaline Adams, 10, and Chris Adams, 61, visited Cooperstown for induction weekend in July 2018.

But I do remember watching him on TV with George Kell. That's my childhood. I'd watch George and Al on the TV, and my dad would be out in the yard with a radio hanging from his belt listening to Ernie Harwell.

I met Kaline for the first time in June 2012. It was my first day on the job as a sports columnist for the Detroit Free Press.

"What do you remember about your first day in the big leagues?" I asked him.

"I was scared to death," Kaline said. "Didn't know anybody. Didn't know where to sit."

His face lit up from the memory. It was June 23, 1953, and the Tigers were playing the Philadelphia Athletics at Connie Mack Stadium in front of 2,463 fans. He was an 18-year-old, straight out of high school.

"My locker was a nail in the bathroom," Kaline said. "That's where I hung my clothes."

Two nights later, he had one at-bat in his debut, in the ninth inning, and he remembered the relief of hitting a fly ball to centerfield. "It was the only day I was glad to make an out," Kaline says, "because I wanted to get back on that bench so fast."

He smiled and laughed.

Here was a man with 3,007 hits. A man with 22 seasons as a big-leaguer. A man with a statue behind the left-center fence at Comerica Park.

And he was as approachable and as friendly as a next-door neighbor.

CONTINUED ON PAGE 37

KIRTHMON F. DOZIER

Four days after the Tigers drafted him fifth overall in June 2019, Riley Greene wowed players, officials and media with his BP power display. After chatting with Riley at the cage, Al Kaline said of the 18-year-old from Florida: "I like everything about him so far. He helped pick the balls up — he didn't act like he's anything special."

CONTINUED FROM PAGE 36

Humble to the end

My team was the '84 Tigers when I was growing up in Bay City, Michigan.

The '68 Tigers were my dad's team. And every time I talked to Kaline, I felt like I was representing my father and his generation.

In 2018, the Tigers kicked off a 50th anniversary celebration of their 1968 World Series title and Kaline talked about that magical season.

"I got hurt," Kaline said, referencing his broken forearm. "I missed a lot of that season. I'm forever grateful to the players that kept playing and played their — pardon my expression — butts off. I will always praise Jim Northrup. The way Jim Northrup went about his business and was an outstanding player that year, I'll never forget that. I'm forever grateful to all the players who battled. Fortunately, I was able to come back and start playing."

He couldn't help but be humble.

While talking about that title, he gave all kinds of praise to the Tigers' bench. "I don't think they get the (recognition) that they should," Kaline said. "They really played a big role in winning the world championship. You have to have 25 players. You can't win with just nine guys."

I never get starstruck talking to current athletes. But it was different talking to Kaline.

It felt like I was talking to Ty Cobb, or some other great from history.

I just held him in reverence. And I could never call him Al.

"Hello, Mr. Kaline," I would say every time I saw him.

He would walk through the Tigers clubhouse, see me, squeeze my forearm and smile. He just made you feel good.

And the coolest thing was watching him at spring training, dressed in a uniform, talking to young Tigers and giving advice. Or just hanging out at the ballpark.

In the summer of 2019, Kaline stood behind a batting cage in Comerica Park, as Riley Greene, the first-round draft pick, was taking batting practice. Greene launched a ball onto the second deck in right-field, and the ball bounced into Kaline's Corner, the seating area named after the spot where Kaline made so many great plays at Tiger Stadium.

To me, it was magical. Like the baseball gods were writing poetry. Just seeing Kaline and Greene interact — Kaline came off the field, praising Greene. Here was a Hall of Famer, excited about the future, excited about the next young kid.

That's the part I'm going to miss the most.

Not just the connection to the past.

But his elegant, humble spirit and the way he made you feel.

Mr. Tiger had the ability to make even the most nervous celebrity feel right at home around him

The star of the show

BY SHAWN WINDSOR

Tom Selleck doesn't get nervous often. But when the actor spotted Al Kaline coming toward him in the spring of 1991, his stomach began knotting up.

Selleck was sitting at his locker stall inside the Tigers' clubhouse in Lakeland, Florida, getting dressed so he could take the field for practice — he was there doing research for a movie called "Mr. Baseball." Suddenly, Kaline pulled up a stool to chat.

"And as I was looking at him, I noticed the players all looking at me," Selleck said. "But Al kept talking, asking how I was doing."

Right about then, Selleck stuck his foot into a cleat — and into a mess of goo. One of his "teammates" had filled his shoe with skin salve. Kaline had come over to distract him.

"He suckered me," Selleck said.

The Detroit-born actor is known almost as much for the Tigers cap he wore on his hit 1980s show, "Magnum, P.I.," as he is for his mustache. The cap is in the Smithsonian, along with the Hawaiian shirt his character sported.

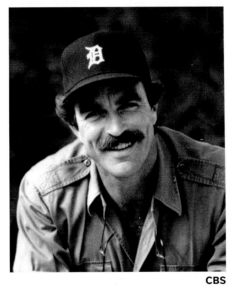

CBS

Detroit-born actor Tom Selleck donned the old English D as private investigator Thomas Magnum for 162 episodes from 1980-88.

As for the mustache? It should probably be there, too.

Kaline joked with him about the mustache and joked with him in general. He made him feel like one of the guys, even as he had to pinch himself that he was chatting with his childhood hero.

"I felt complimented," Selleck said, especially when the guys put IcyHot in his jockstrap.

No, that wasn't Kaline, though the legendary Tiger got a kick out of hearing about it. Yet humor and pranks weren't the reason Selleck wanted to talk about Kaline.

"I thought the nation should know a little more about who he was," Selleck said. "He's a huge loss. So active in the formation of so many players. Such an influence. You always wished you had more time with someone like that."

Selleck, at 75 still starring on TV with the police drama "Blue Bloods," was devastated by Kaline's passing. He was his favorite player.

"I'd see him on the game of the week sometimes," he said, after his family had left Detroit in 1948 for Los Angeles, where he still lived.

He got to see Kaline play in person, too, when the family packed up the car to drive across the country to visit relatives. They drove straight through because Selleck's father made his money selling real estate and didn't get paid if he couldn't earn commission. So he bolted across the country as fast as he could.

Every summer back in Detroit, Selleck would go to a Tigers game. He once got into the clubhouse and managed to meet Kaline.

CONTINUED ON PAGE 39

JULIAN H. GONZALEZ

In August 1992, Tom Selleck threw out Bernie Carbo in the Upper Deck Heroes of Baseball exhibition at Tiger Stadium. The 1972 ALCS heroes (Tigers, Athletics and Selleck) played the 1972 NLCS heroes (Pirates and Reds). Alas, the NL triumphed, 4-0. "Mr. Baseball," which did $40 million at the box office, received mixed reviews.

CONTINUED FROM PAGE 38

He was 10 or 11.

"I just admired him as a ballplayer," Selleck said. "The way he played, with a kind of grace and dignity and commitment. The way he moved, cruising around rightfield. He looked like he was just loping after a ball down the rightfield line, until he hit the stands, and he'd tumble over, and I'd realize how fast he was traveling."

Because of those trips back to Michigan, and because Los Angeles didn't have a baseball team — the Dodgers didn't move there from Brooklyn until after the 1957 season — the Tigers were always his team.

And when he got the role of Thomas Magnum and knew the character needed to wear a baseball cap, the choice was obvious.

For a stretch in the '80s, he helped make the cap MLB's top-seller.

"I've always been very proud of that," Selleck said.

'Looked up to him'

As Selleck's fame grew — he made a few hit movies as well — he got more opportunities to spend time with Kaline. But it wasn't until his movie prep for "Mr. Baseball" took him to spring training that he really got to know Kaline.

One day, while he was stretching on the field, Kaline approached him and asked him to play catch.

"Long toss," Selleck said.

Again, he tried to keep his cool. It helped that he'd lived as a celebrity for more than a decade and knew better than to ask a lot of questions. He had worked with other famous actors and was accustomed to being around the buzz (although he admits he had to stay calm the first time he met Faye Dunaway).

Playing catch and chatting with Kaline was different, though. Childhood awe can stick with you in that way.

"I just tried to have regular conversation," Selleck said.

About baseball. The Tigers. Life.

Before Selleck finished his apprenticeship that spring, Sparky Anderson, the Tigers' manager, told him he was going to give him an at-bat. One day, the Reds came to town. They were the defending World Series champions. One of their closers, Rob Dibble, threw high-90s heat and was known for an intense, scowling presence on the mound.

It was the seventh inning when Anderson called upon Selleck to grab a bat. Just then, Dibble entered the game. Anderson, not wanting to get the 6-foot-4 Selleck killed, told him to wait.

The next inning, Selleck took his stance in the batter's box against a more predictable pitcher. He struck out. "But I fouled off four pitches," he said.

He hadn't made a fool of himself in front of his idol. He still remembered the feeling.

That's how it is with heroes, even if you're a kind of hero yourself. No matter how much your fame grows, you can never outgrow the view you had as a child.

For Selleck, and for so many others who loved the Tigers, Kaline was the shooting star, gliding across the galaxy.

"I looked up to him," Selleck said. "And I'm proud to say I knew him."

Kaline made sure the lessons he learned as a Tiger were passed from generation to generation

Class was in session

BY ANTHONY FENECH

Somewhere, probably boxed up in Kirk Gibson's basement, there is a VHS tape of Al Kaline dancing.

It is from 1985, at the Detroit Yacht Club, as Gibson and longtime Tigers teammate Dave Rozema married the Sklarski sisters in a dual ceremony "that may never be matched in the annals of baseball," the Chicago Tribune wrote at the time.

"You should see him dancing out there," Gibson recalled a few days after Kaline's death at 85.

It is one of the most vivid memories Gibson has of Kaline, a man he grew up idolizing as a youngster in Waterford, Michigan, and a man Gibson credited with making him a rightfielder. They shared a certain bond and friendship as two of the most identifiable figures in Tigers history.

"Getting to be around him and understanding who he was on and off the field, it was pretty incredible," Gibson said. "Like I told people, he treated me better than I should have been, probably. He was like Sparky

JULIAN H. GONZALEZ

Manager Alan Trammell and Al Kaline found something amusing in Lakeland in 2003. "As a young player," Trammell said, "if you asked him a question, he would give you great information. ... He was certainly one of my mentors."

(Anderson) in that they're hell-bent on making sure the game is better than it was when they came in. That's their big deal."

Lessons in Lakeland

Kaline was the Tigers' all-time franchise player and when he came across people, they were better for it. When I saw a picture of Kaline sitting by himself on a bench on the back

fields of Tiger Town, it prompted my most vivid memory of Mr. Tiger.

Early in my sportswriting career, I sat next to Kaline for a couple of those spring training days in Lakeland, Florida, asking him questions about hitting and the game and how it had evolved. Once he recognized my face, I'd walk up to chat with him. For the first few years, it helped that

CONTINUED ON PAGE 41

Kirk Gibson and Al Kaline — Tigers rightfielders present and past — talked shop in Lakeland, Florida, during spring training in 1986. Now a Tigers broadcaster, Gibson said after Kaline's death: "A lot of the stuff I talk about on TV, that's Kaline."

CONTINUED FROM PAGE 40
his good friend and former teammate Jim Price approved of me as a "rookie."

There are thousands of these stories about Kaline, passed along from generation to generation of Tigers fans. Stories of humility, of respect, of a boyhood idol who was even better in person, as Gibson learned on those same back fields in Tiger Town.

"He taught me virtually everything," Gibson said. "Ninety-plus percent of what I knew out there.

"He was really a kind of easy-going guy with most people. But this guy competed. I'm telling you, he didn't want to be mediocre. He wanted it all. He wanted to win. He wanted you to give everything that you could give him."

Gibson remembered the last time he talked to Kaline, in spring 2020, at a Chili's in an "Only in Tiger Town" scene. He was sitting at the bar with Alan Trammell when they saw Kaline and his wife, Louise, in a booth around the corner.

"If you ever had somebody die that you know, a friend or somebody special and you say to yourself, 'I wish I would have said something I didn't

say,'" Gibson said, "that's something I never really ever want to happen. Don't let that happen. If you're with that conversation, man, don't go and force it, but you really gotta put yourself in that situation. It will happen with people like that."

Gibson saw firsthand Kaline's bond with modern-day players. "He loved all of these guys, man," Gibson said. "I just hope they know it. I hope they realized the treasure."

Asked whether he realized the treasure, Gibson quickly replied: "Oh, yeah. There's so many of them."

The cat's meow **41**

Mr. Tiger & Mr. Hockey shared a love for the links

Two of a kind

BY GEORGE SIPPLE AND MARK SNYDER

Throughout the 1950s and 1960s, the two iconic sports stars in Detroit were right wing Gordie Howe of the Red Wings and rightfielder Al Kaline of the Tigers. During their Hall of Fame careers, they became fast friends.

Howe joined the Wings as an 18-year-old in 1946. He retired at 43 in 1971. Kaline joined the Tigers as an 18-year-old in 1953. He retired at 39 in 1974.

Howe won his first NHL scoring title with 86 points (43 goals, 43 assists) as a 22-year-old in 1951, 20 points ahead of runner-up Maurice (Rocket) Richard. Kaline won his American League batting title at .340 as a 20-year-old in 1955, 21 points ahead of runner-up Vic Power.

In an interview with the Free Press shortly before Howe suffered a serious stroke in October 2014, Kaline reflected on his relationship with Howe:

▢ "Gordie's one of a kind. Of course, his nickname, Mr. Hockey, is exactly what he is. Other than the fact he was a great, great, great hockey player, he is one of the great people that I've ever run into in sports. Our friendship has gone back a long ways. We lived at one time close to each other."

▢ "I used to go to hockey games with a friend of both of ours and afterwards we would go to Carl's steakhouse — which is no longer there —

after the game before we went home. Several other players and their wives were always there, too. That's how I ran into Gordie."

▢ "Gordie would come down to the ballpark once in a while and maybe take batting practice with us at that time in Briggs Stadium. When we started to go to dinner, we got very friendly."

In the late '50s, Kaline and Howe started a business with Frank Carlin, one of Howe's friends and a businessman from Birmingham, Michigan. It was called Michigan Automotive Products Corporation, with Howe as president, Kaline as vice president and Carlin as treasurer and general manager. In "The Al Kaline Story," a 1964 book, author Al Hirshberg described their venture this way: "With the two athletes making the contacts and Carlin closing the deals, the business began prospering almost immediately. Soon the trio formed Howe-Kaline-Carlin Corporation, manufacturers' representatives. Its insignia was a crossed baseball bat and hockey stick. This was a separate business, which also did well.

"Much to his surprise, Al found that he enjoyed selling. It took some time for him to feel completely at ease with people, but he learned to relax because he had to. Selling was a challenge which he likened to playing ball. Each new customer was a new pitcher, presenting problems that had to be solved. He had to talk in order to overcome them. While he never became a chatterbox, he was no longer the clam he had been."

Howe, Kaline and Carlin also

formed HKC Stables after the 1959 baseball season. Horses with names such as Stormy Al, Challenge Baby and Birthday Mage won a few races in Toledo, Ohio, before heading to Detroit Race Course in May 1960. That's when the Detroit newspapers got wind of it and a bit of a fuss erupted for a short while because of baseball's uneasy alliance with gambling. Kaline quickly sold his share to Carlin. Howe had backed out months before him, Kaline said, because he "didn't like horses enough or have enough interest in racing."

Kaline, like an estimated 15,000 others in June 2016, paid his respects to Howe at a public visitation inside Joe Louis Arena four days after his old pal died. Mr. Hockey was 88. Mr. Tiger, then 81, told more stories about their time together — on the golf course, on the diamond, on the ice and in the public eye.

"I got to be very friendly with Gordie and played golf with him, mostly at Plum Hollow, and he was a very good golfer," Kaline said. "I just started playing, and he put up with me for a while."

Kaline's game quickly improved, so much so that he later became a member at Oakland Hills Country Club, the most prestigious course in the state.

Kaline invited Howe to Briggs Stadium for a little BP.

"He had trouble hitting it for a while," Kaline said. "Then he hit one over the fence, and it was like he scored the winning goal in the playoffs."

CONTINUED ON PAGE 43

Tigers rightfielder Al Kaline and Red Wings right wing Gordie Howe, pausing under a tree at Plum Hollow in Southfield, Michigan, were the biggest stars in the Motor City in the 1950s and 1960s — and darn good golfers for decades longer.

CONTINUED FROM PAGE 42

Then Howe returned the favor at Olympia Stadium.

"I never skated before in my life," Kaline said. "I was a one-leg pusher on skates and holding onto the railing, and Gordie being Gordie came over and gave me one of his famous elbows.

"But he was a super person."

The Kalines and the Howes spent a lot of private time in each other's homes. When they were in public together, Kaline saw what he considered a real star.

"Certainly, Gordie was a much bigger name than me," Kaline said, "but people were always nice to us, maybe because of the personality. Gordie was so easy, so pleasant to be around. They showed respect, mostly for Gordie, which they should have."

Detroit was king of the NFL in the 1950s, but even those football stars looked up to Mr. Tiger

Pride of the Lions

BY DAVE BIRKETT

O f all the pieces of memorabilia Joe Schmidt had from his playing days with the Detroit Lions, one picture stood above the rest.

Sometime in the 1950s, Schmidt, the Pro Football Hall of Fame linebacker, attended a sports banquet in Detroit with Tigers outfielder Al Kaline and Red Wings forward Gordie Howe.

The three posed for a picture, with Schmidt in front, Howe in the middle and Kaline in back. Schmidt tracked down a copy of the photo after it ran in a local paper, had his Detroit sports contemporaries autograph it, and for the past 60 or so years, it's hung in a frame somewhere in his house.

"I couldn't hold a stick to either one of those in regards to ability," Schmidt said the day Kaline passed. "All I did was jump on piles and Al hit a baseball and Gordie hit the puck skating. It was a different sport altogether than what I was doing. Mine was just knocking people around."

Joe Moreau, 76, of Livonia, Michigan, proudly showed off his framed copy of the Schmidt-Howe-Kaline photograph, a signed duplicate given to him by Lions Hall of Fame linebacker Joe Schmidt, his employer for 35 years as a manufacturer's representative in the automotive business.
SHARON MOREAU

Schmidt, a seventh-round draft pick, played for the Lions from 1953-65, winning NFL championships in 1953 and 1957, and coached the Lions from 1967-72, compiling a 43-34-7 record with one playoff loss.

Schmidt, at 88, and other Lions greats remembered Mr. Tiger as a distinguished baseball player and a man of class.

"He was special," linebacker Mike Lucci said. "He was a cut above."

Lucci and Kaline hung out occa

sionally during their playing days and saw each other more often in retirement as members at Oakland Hills Country Club.

Kaline took part in a few of Lucci's charity golf outings, and Lucci said the two sometimes would joke about the money they made as players and how it compared to the salaries for players these days.

"He told me the story one time of when he first got to $100,000 and I

CONTINUED ON PAGE 45

Longtime member Al Kaline and Lions quarterback Jon Kitna walked the 18th fairway at Oakland Hills Country Club in July 2007. A celebrity scramble kicked off ticket sales for 2008's PGA Championship (which Padraig Harrington would win).

CONTINUED FROM PAGE 44
guess he batted .299 or whatever it was, it wasn't like the year before," Lucci said. "And they wanted to cut his pay. I told him, I said if you were playing today they'd have to give you half the team."

Kaline made his major-league debut in 1953 as an 18-year old, while Lucci played the 1965-73 seasons with the Lions. The teams were based at Tiger Stadium.

"We were obviously playing at the same place and we rooted for him," Lucci said. "Probably ran around with some of the other ones a little more than him. He was a little quieter, or stayed out of public a little bit. But I've known him since the '60s and he was always classy."

Schmidt called Kaline "a class guy," too. They were acquaintances more than close friends. They ran into each other at banquets a few times during their playing days and several times after when they were in the automobile business, and he said he never heard Kaline utter a bad word about anyone.

That's another reason why he cherished the photo that sat in the TV room of his Florida home. Kaline never bragged about his accomplishments. Neither did Howe. They carried themselves like the winners they were.

"When you're good like those two guys, you don't have to brag," Schmidt said. "Everybody knows about it."

And nobody forgets it.

Kaline's corner

3

6

Al Kaline covered a lot of ground as a Tiger, from starring at The Corner to serving as the elder statesman of the franchise. Through it all, he kept Detroit up to date with a series of newspaper columns. Here is his baseball life, in his own words.

On Aug. 17, 1980, Al Kaline stepped to the microphone and told fans he was "one of the luckiest baseball players that ever lived." That day the Tigers retired his uniform No. 6, two weeks after his induction into the Hall of Fame.
ALAN R. KAMUDA

No player spent more time at The Corner than Mr. Tiger — 1,421 regular-season games

Corner office

BY AL KALINE

Al Kaline reflected on his memories of Tiger Stadium for "The Corner," a Free Press book released in 1999, the old ballpark's final season.

I became a Tiger in June 1953, when I was 18. I joined the team in Philadelphia and then went to Washington, then came to Detroit. At that time we landed at Willow Run Airport and took a bus back to Detroit. We came down Michigan Avenue. I was sitting next to Johnny Pesky and he said, "Now I'm going to show you what Briggs Stadium looks like."

It was about 1 or 2 o'clock in the morning and he said, "It's going to look like a big ol' battleship." And sure enough, I looked out there through the darkness and it looked like a big ol' battleship.

Pesky said, "We call it 'The Old Lady.'"

The next day was the first time I went into the stadium. I was staying downtown at the Wolverine Hotel and I walked to the park with a guy named Johnny Bucha, a catcher. I walked out on the field right away, before I went into the locker room, and it was all green. It was unbelievable how beautiful it was. All the seats were green. It was magnificent. I'd never seen anything like it being just out of high school.

Of course, since I was a kid they put me in the last locker all the way in the back. They had very few young guys at the time. Everybody spent a lot of time in the minor leagues before they got a chance at the majors, so I wasn't greeted too well. We had a lot of guys who were 26 or 27 years old, and that seemed pretty old to me at the time.

When I first joined the club, we only had 12 or 14 night games a year. It was amazing; every time — it didn't matter whether it was the Washington Senators or the New York Yankees — we had a full house. We had 50,000 people.

Maybe my biggest memory there was of hitting three home runs in one game, two in the same inning, one Sunday afternoon against the A's in 1955.

And I remember Reggie Jackson hitting a home run in the '71 All-Star Game. You had to know the situation in that game. He had two strikes on him, and to be that aggressive with two strikes is just phenomenal. Boy, when he hit that ball and it went all the way out there to the transformer, I didn't believe it. He hit it off Dock Ellis.

Of course, there are a lot of memories, too, after I quit playing and began broadcasting.

I had a difficult time at first, no

CONTINUED ON PAGE 49

For 22 seasons, Al Kaline plied his trade at Michigan and Trumbull. In June 1953, his teammates told him the stadium looked like a battleship. In September 1999, Kaline took Detroit's lineup card to home plate in Tiger Stadium's final game. DETROIT FREE PRESS

CONTINUED FROM PAGE 48
question about it, because a lot of the guys on the team were still my friends. There were three guys in the booth, and I didn't know when to talk. The "professional" announcer would say something about the game and even though I thought it was wrong, I didn't correct it and sort of let it ride. But I finally decided I couldn't do that, that I had to correct it and say exactly what I thought was going on,

When the team moves, it's going to be very sad for me personally because Tiger Stadium's the only place I've ever worked — every summer of my life since I've been out of high school.

Al Kaline played his first game at Briggs Stadium on July 16, 1953. He pinch ran for Bob Nieman at first base with one out in the ninth and the Tigers trailing Boston, 3-2. Pinch-hitter Steve (Bud) Souchock then grounded into a 4-6-3 double play. Kaline played his final game at Tiger Stadium on Oct. 2, 1974. As the DH, he struck out looking in the first inning and flied out to left in the third inning. He was replaced by pinch-hitter Ben Oglivie in the fifth inning of what would be a 5-4 loss to Baltimore.

Home cooking

Al Kaline is the career leader in games, plate appearances, hits, homers, RBIs and walks at Briggs/Tiger Stadium. Here's how his regular-season stats at the corner of Michigan and Trumbull stack up against his stats on the road:

Category	Home	Away
Plate appearances	5,732	5,864
At-bats	4,984	5,132
Hits	1,508	1,499
Home runs	226	173
RBIs	827	755
Walks	648	628

The Tigers and Cardinals stood at attention in October 1968 when the World Series returned to Detroit for the first time since 1945. That year, the Tigers beat the Chicago Cubs in seven games.
DETROIT FREE PRESS

After 17 seasons, Mr. Tiger finally reached the top

Champions, at last!

BY GENE MYERS

During the 1968 World Series, Tigers rightfielder Al Kaline penned a daily column for the Free Press. He chronicled the highest of highs — his first World Series, his hit that turned the tide in Game 5, Detroit's first world championship in 23 years — and the lowest of lows — his three-strikeout game, a 10-1 embarrassment at Tiger Stadium, the three-games-to-one deficit.

In his first column, filed before Game 1 in St. Louis, Kaline discussed manager Mayo Smith's bold gamble: moving cen-

CONTINUED ON PAGE 52

JUNFU HAN

In September 2018, at a 50th reunion of the World Series champions, the Tigers presented each player a scale-sized replica of the 1968 trophy. Catcher Bill Freehan, selected for the All-Star Game from 1964-73, wore the No. 11 uniform.

CONTINUED FROM PAGE 51
terfielder Mickey Stanley to shortstop for light-hitting Ray Oyler so that Kaline could play in right.

Kaline wrote: *"It surprised me and I appreciate Mickey Stanley even trying to do the job at shortstop. I know there'll be great pressure on him — it's tough enough in just a regular-season game let alone the World Series. ...*

"I've waited 16 years for this day. ... I just hope I will play well enough that Mayo will have to play me in the second game."

In Game 1, Bob Gibson, who finished the season with a 1.12 ERA, struck out 17 Tigers, a World Series record, in a 4-0 five-hitter on Oct. 2. Kaline doubled but, like Norm Cash, struck out three times. He was Gibson's second, eighth and, in the ninth inning, 15th strikeout victim (which tied Sandy Koufax's Series record set in 1963). Gibson ended the game by fanning Cash and Willie Horton.

Kaline wrote: *"It was just too much Gibson. We weren't surprised that he threw as hard as he did, but we were* surprised that his slider was so good. I think he's one of the greatest pitchers I've ever faced. I feel good that I was able to get a hit off him. The pitchers have a definite advantage in a series like this and, of course, he's something else. ...

"The last time up he threw all fastballs. We weren't aware that he was going for a strikeout record and I guess we were as surprised as he was. ...

"I'm happy that it worked out at shortstop — Mickey Stanley played it really well there and got two hits. Mickey did so well that I understand we're going with the same lineup and I'll be in rightfield again. Now we've got to get them in the second game."

In Game 2, Horton, Mickey Lolich and Cash belted solo home runs, Kaline singled twice and scored twice, and Lolich went the distance with nine strikeouts in an 8-1 victory.

Kaline wrote: *"How about that Mickey Lolich? I told him I'm not going to let him use my bats anymore — he's taking all the hits out of them. Mickey used one of my bats Thursday* and you know what happened — he hit his first home run in pro ball and then singled later in the game and went 2-for-4.

"He liked the bat so much he took it home with him, and I guess I won't see that one again. But I'd be happy to give him the whole rack of bats if he keeps that up."

In Game 3, the first World Series game in Detroit since 1945, Kaline's

CONTINUED ON PAGE 53

A bleak situation in Game 5 — the Tigers trailed the Cardinals, three games to one — turned far worse when Orlando Cepeda smacked a two-run homer in the first inning for a 3-0 St. Louis lead. Left-hander Mickey Lolich blamed his rocky start on the umpires cutting short his pregame warm-up time.
DETROIT FREE PRESS

CONTINUED FROM PAGE 52

two-run homer gave the Tigers a lead in the third inning. But three steals from Lou Brock and three-run homers by Tim McCarver and Orlando Cepeda produced a 7-3 St. Louis victory.

Kaline wrote: *"There's no question about it. We're not in real great shape having to go against Bob Gibson and being down in the Series, two games to one. Gibson is one of the greatest pitchers I've ever seen. ...*

"Lou Brock ... I wish he'd catch a cold or something. I've never seen anyone disrupt a game the way he does. I get a pretty good shot at him from rightfield, and I've never seen anyone with so much speed on the first step. ...

"I really appreciated that standing ovation from the fans in right and center. I've never had an ovation like that in my 16 years in Detroit. It made me feel great."

In Game 4, a horrible, rainy affair, Tigers fans chanted for more rain so that the game wouldn't become official. More rain came but the game sloshed on nonetheless as the Cardinals won, 10-1, for a three-games-to-one advantage. Brock led off the day with a deep homer off Denny McLain, who surrendered four early runs, didn't return after a third-in-

CONTINUED ON PAGE 54

Al Kaline went down the line greeting his 1968 teammates, including Willie Horton, during a 50th reunion in September 2018. Thirteen players attended at Comerica Park: Kaline, Horton, Wayne Comer, John Hiller, Mickey Lolich, Tom Matchick, Denny McLain, Daryl Patterson, Jim Price, Mickey Stanley, Dick Tracewski, Jon Warden and Don Wert.

CONTINUED FROM PAGE 53

ning rain delay and said afterward his season was over because of a sore right shoulder. The Tigers didn't hit (Gibson struck 10), didn't pitch (the bullpen gave up six runs, including a homer by Gibson and a bases-loaded walk to Gibson) and didn't field (Bill Freehan, Eddie Mathews, Jim Northrup and McLain committed errors).

Kaline wrote: *"Well, it was a complete team effort. We played as a team all year and we did it again Sunday only it was in reverse. This was the worst game we played all season and one of the worst we've played in the 16 years I've been with the club. We didn't get the pitching and our defense was ragged. The poor defense contributed to the pitching breakdown. Denny McLain's arm obviously bothers him. ...*

"I wasn't surprised that they restarted the game after the rain. I knew that if we started, we'd play it out no matter what. We did everything we could to stall it but it didn't work. And weren't those fans something? I've never heard anything like that in baseball — they were cheering for rain."

In Game 5, with Lolich on the mound trying to save the season, the Cardinals led, 3-0, after four batters. But they never scored again. The entire series changed in the middle innings.

In the bottom of the fourth, Stanley and Horton tripled and Cash and Northrup supplied the RBIs. In the top of the fifth, Horton fielded Julian Javier's single to left, threw to Freehan at the plate and nailed Brock, who chose not to slide. In the bottom of the seventh, the Tigers loaded the bases with one out for Kaline — Lolich on third, Dick McAuliffe on second, Stanley on first. Kaline looped the ball on the fly into short right-center, a two-hopper to center-fielder Curt Flood, scoring Lolich and McAuliffe. "It sent goose pimples all over my back," Kaline said later, "and it was a tremendous thrill to think that I was able to do something for the fans after all these years." From 3-2 down to 4-3 up, the Tigers had the lead and actually would never

CONTINUED ON PAGE 55

The 1968 World Series turned in Game 5 when Willie Horton's throw from left to Bill Freehan cut down Lou Brock, who shockingly did not slide.
TONY SPINA

CONTINUED FROM PAGE 54
trail again in the World Series.

George Cantor wrote in the Free Press: "Trailing by one run in the seventh, the team pulled it out in the late innings for the 41st time this season. And they never did it in a bigger one. Al Kaline justified all the position shuffling once and for all as he sent home the two decisive runs with a bases-loaded single in one of the most dramatic moments in the history of the park. The light towers swayed as the crowd of 53,634 roared their tribute to the longtime hero, enjoying his greatest moments in the Series for which he waited so long."

With a 5-3 lead and one on and one out in the ninth inning, Lolich surrendered a single to pinch-hitter Ed Spiezio, who had fouled off eight straight pitches. But Lolich ended the game by striking out pinch-hitter Roger Maris and retiring Brock, who already

had three hits off him, on a check-swing two-hopper to the mound that Lolich sky-underhanded the entire distance to first baseman Cash.

Kaline wrote: *"That wasn't one of my hardest hits, but it was one of the sweetest ones. I just was trying to get a base hit — hit it up the middle or hit a fly to center, just to get the run in from third to tie the game. I felt if we tied it, we'd win it. Joe Hoerner has been pitching me fastballs away all the time and I was*

looking for it. I didn't try to pull it because I might hit into a double play. I wasn't excited or nervous. I enjoy hitting with men on base. I don't have as much incentive with nobody on.

"It's difficult to say how much winning that game meant and the ovation the fans gave me when I went back to rightfield. They've been so good to me and to us that we just couldn't lose all three games in our park. We couldn't let the American League down, but even more we couldn't let the fans down. ...

"Before the game, Norm Cash and I went around and talked to the guys, trying to keep their spirits up. Norm is the fun guy on the club and I'm the serious one. We've been together a long time. We told them to swing for base hits and not home runs, to go out there and have some fun. I love these kind of conditions — the crowd and the pressure — and I'm going to fight like hell the rest of the way."

In Game 6, back in St. Louis, McLain returned to the mound despite only two days' rest and an inflamed tendon in his right shoulder. A shot of cortisone and xylocaine proved to be a magic elixir. A 31-game winner, McLain finally won in the World Series, scattering nine hits, striking out seven, walking none, surviving a 49-minute rain delay in the eighth inning and coming within an out of a shutout.

But the Tigers' offense was the bigger story: Detroit scored 10 runs in the third inning en route to a 13-1 series-tying victory. The Tigers paraded 15 men to the plate in the big inning. The Cardinals needed a record-tying four pitchers to get them out. Northrup belted the 11th grand slam in Series history; he had four such homers during the season. Kaline

CONTINUED ON PAGE 56

CONTINUED FROM PAGE 55

and Cash became the 14th and 15th players to collect two hits in the same inning. The 10-run explosion equaled the output of the 1929 Philadelphia Athletics, who wiped out an 8-0 deficit in the seventh inning of Game 4 to shock the Cubs. (In the next game, the A's scored three times in the bottom of the ninth to shock the Cubs again, 3-2, to win the championship.)

Kaline singled twice in the third, driving in three runs, and hit a solo homer off Steve Carlton in the fifth. The Tigers got a scare in the eighth when an inside pitch from Wayne Granger caught Kaline on the left elbow. He rubbed it, trotted down the line and touched first base for the fourth time.

Kaline wrote: *"Now it's down to us against Bob Gibson. I've said all along that if we lose, I'd rather it be to Gibson — and I wanted it to go to seven games. We're at seven games now, and we've got a chance to beat them. We've got momentum going, but winning, 13-1, doesn't make us a better ballclub; what it does is make them think a little more about us.*

"St. Louis has a great club. I don't think they'll be rattled by that game — they're too good to be rattled. ...

"It seems like we always get a big inning for Denny, and I understand this one tied a World Series record that's stood since 1929. I got two singles in that inning, and I was just trying to advance the runners the first time up, like in Monday's game in Detroit. I hit the ball a little bit better this time to centerfield.

"I hit a real good curveball, down and in, for a home run in the fifth, and I certainly have no complaints about not getting my hits in this Series."

In Game 7, Lolich started on two days' rest, Gibson on three days' rest for the second time. Yet, neither team came close to scoring through six innings on Oct. 10, 1968. Stanley was the Tigers' lone runner, reaching on an infield single to shortstop in the

DETROIT FREE PRESS

Like Al Kaline, the Tigers were knocked down by the Cardinals but refused to stay down. He hit .379 with two homers and eight RBIs. Joe Falls wrote in the Free Press: "No longer does our city have to be the butt of a lot of bad jokes. No longer can they poke fun at our baseball team."

fourth. Lolich dealt with men on base in three of the first five innings but only one reached second base. In the sixth inning, Brock led off with a single but Lolich picked him off, throwing to first as Brock broke for second. Cash fired to Stanley, who applied the tag with a nary a nanosecond to spare. With two outs, Flood singled and Lolich picked him off, trapping Flood off first and ending the inning with a 1-3-4-1-6 rundown.

In the top of the seventh, Gibson had retired 20 of the Tigers' 21 batters. Then, with two outs, Cash and Horton singled. Flood, a Gold Glove centerfielder, misjudged Northrup's drive to center, stumbled and allowed a triple that scored Cash and Horton. Freehan, who started the series 0-for-16, doubled home Northrup for a 3-0 lead.

Lolich needed nine more outs for his third complete-game victory and Detroit's first World Series championship since 1945. He worked around a Northrup error in the seventh and

a walk to Brock in the eighth. He surrendered a two-out homer in the ninth to Mike Shannon, losing a shutout with one out to go, just as McLain had done in Game 6. But Lolich easily retired McCarver on a foul pop to Freehan — and then jumped into his catcher's arms.

With their 4-1 victory, Tigers became the third team to overcome a 3-1 World Series deficit. Lolich, with a 3-0 record and a 1.67 ERA, was voted the most valuable player. Kaline finished with a .379 average (11-for-29), a hit in every game but the last, eight RBIs, two homers, two doubles and six runs.

Kaline wrote about Game 7: *"It always means more when you have to work for something and, of course, I've been around 16 years and this is my first pennant and first Series.*

"And then, the way we won it made it doubly good, the way we played all year. ...

"It's been my greatest year in baseball. I'll never forget it."

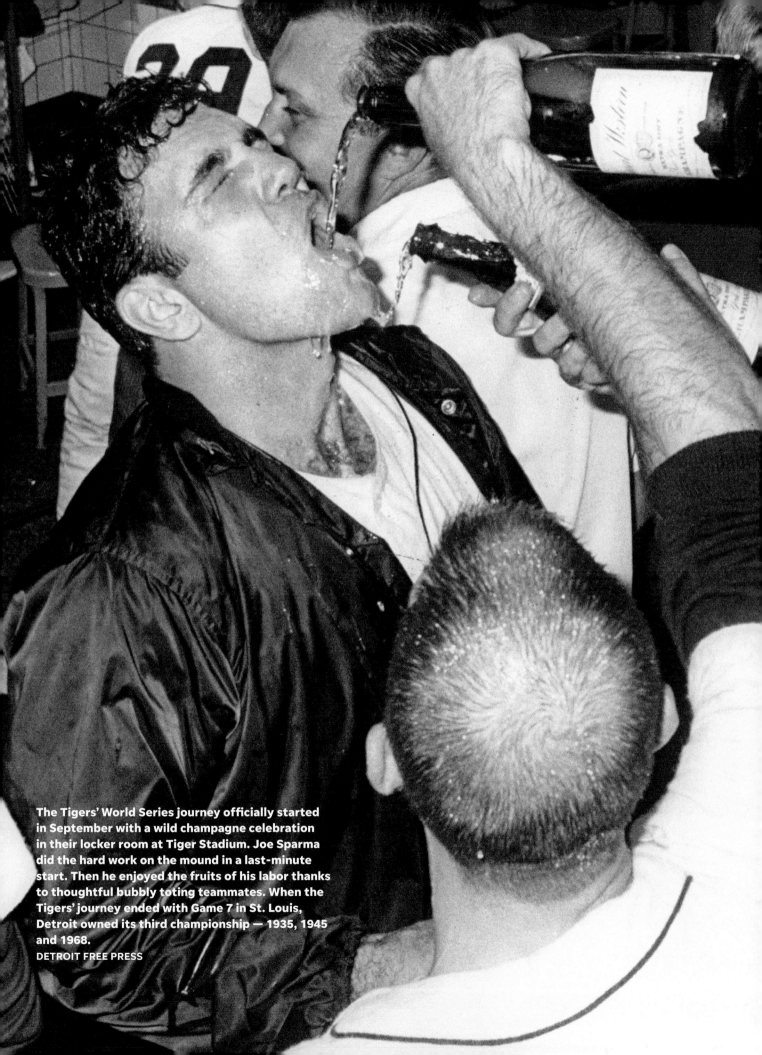

The Tigers' World Series journey officially started in September with a wild champagne celebration in their locker room at Tiger Stadium. Joe Sparma did the hard work on the mound in a last-minute start. Then he enjoyed the fruits of his labor thanks to thoughtful bubbly toting teammates. When the Tigers' journey ended with Game 7 in St. Louis, Detroit owned its third championship — 1935, 1945 and 1968.
DETROIT FREE PRESS

Just hours after he and the Tigers had won the World Series, Kaline's thoughts on beating the Cardinals were already on their way to readers

Arm and hammer

BY AL KALINE

Tigers rightfielder Al Kaline wrote a daily column for the Free Press during the 1968 World Series. He filed his final column on Oct. 10, 1968, not long after the Tigers' 4-1 victory in Game 7 in St. Louis. Here's Kaline's piece in its entirety as it ran in the next day's editions.

We had our strongest arm going for us and he won it and we won it the way we have all year, by coming from behind.

Mickey Lolich's arm is the strongest on the staff. It's never sore the day after he pitches, the way it is for most pitchers, so I thought he could do a good job even though he had only two days' rest.

Mickey didn't pitch as many innings this season as Bob Gibson, so I think he had an advantage there even though Gibson had the three days' rest.

I was surprised that Mickey had such good control, though. We had to have the well-pitched game and he gave it to us.

Gibson was great again. I think he was better against me than he was in the first game when he struck me out three times. I got a hit in that one but he shut me out this time.

He had a couple of bad breaks — Jim Northrup's ball that went over Curt Flood's head was the big one — and when you've got a tight ball game going like this, you've got to have the breaks and we got them.

I said after the first game that Gibson was one of the best pitchers I've ever faced — after seeing him three times I've got to say he's the greatest.

I can see how Flood had trouble with Jim's ball. In Busch Stadium, on a warm day when people are in shirtsleeves, it's hard to see a line drive come off the bat. And besides that, the field was in poor condition because of the football game they played here Sunday.

At the start of the Series, I remembered what Tony Kubek said about playing in the World Series, that you'll never be as nervous in your life as you are before the first game … until the seventh game and then it's worse.

The worse for me, and I think all of us, was the first game. After that we settled down. I wasn't very nervous today. There wasn't the wild celebration in the clubhouse that we had after winning the pennant, but inside I was as happy and excited.

It always means more when you have to work for something and, of course, I've been around 16 years and this is my first pennant and first Series.

And then, the way we won it made it doubly good, the way we played all year, from the time of that nine-game winning streak right after we lost on Opening Day.

It's been my greatest year in baseball. I'll never forget it.

If not for Tigers left-hander Mickey Lolich, Al Kaline quite likely would have been voted the MVP of the 1968 World Series. Kaline batted .379 with a hit in each game but the last, two homers and eight RBIs. Lolich, though, won three times — twice in do-or-die games. Each victory was a complete game. He posted a 1.67 ERA and a 0.936 WHIP. Plus, a notoriously poor batsman, Lolich hit his first homer as a pro, reached base three other times (two singles and a walk) and scored twice.

MALCOLM EMMONS

Bleacher report

Al Kaline was a hero to a generation of Michiganders, but his legacy stretched far beyond that. Upon his passing, tributes rolled in from players, politicians, media members and celebrities, all of whom called themselves his fans. Here are their words.

What a ticket it would have been: rightfielder Al Kaline, a 1980 Hall of Fame inductee, noted as calm, cool and collected, at the top of the ticket and pitcher Mark (The Bird) Fidrych, the 1976 rookie of the year, noted as bat-crap crazy, as his veep.

DETROIT FREE PRESS

From the grandstands

COMPILED BY BILL DOW, CHRIS THOMAS AND KIRKLAND CRAWFORD

When the Detroit Free Press broke the news of Al Kaline's death on April 6, 2020, tributes began flooding in from across the world via news reports, personal tales and Twitter. Here is a selection of the words from celebrities who adored Mr. Tiger:

MICKEY LOLICH, TIGERS TEAMMATE, 1963-74: "I can tell you he saved my ass a few times pulling in some home run balls."

JOHNNY BENCH, HALL OF FAME CATCHER FOR THE CINCINNATI REDS: "It was a privilege to have known and shared time with Al Kaline, one of the finest men to play the game and walk among us. I talked to him March 27 and got to tell him I loved him."

REGGIE JACKSON, HALL OF FAME SLUGGER: "I thought Al Kaline was the class of the American League along with Brooks Robinson, Frank Robinson and Carl Yastrzemski. Al never made a mistake. I had such admiration for him. He had such a graceful style; it was Joe DiMaggio-like."

ALAN TRAMMELL, HALL OF FAME TIGERS SHORTSTOP: "I have him on a pedestal. That's just how I was raised. Al Kaline is at another level, as far as I'm concerned. Just a special, special

PATRICIA BECK

Al Kaline and Bob Seger chatted in 2000 at the Detroit Golf Club before a fundraiser for the Isiah Thomas Foundation.

person that will obviously never be forgotten but will be sorely missed."

DENNY MCLAIN, TIGERS TEAMMATE, 1963-70: "He was the best I ever saw on an everyday basis. He knew everything that was going on in a game and what he had to do to make sure our ballclub won. I never saw a better outfielder and he had the most accurate arm. He was such a clutch hitter. Everything he did was with class and he never showed anybody up."

DEBBIE DINGELL, U.S. CONGRESSWOMAN (D-DEARBORN): "From being my hero as a teenager watching the Tigers win the World Series, to the days

that Al Kaline became my friend after I married John, he was one of the most decent human beings I knew. Kind, gentile, real, with great stories. Heaven welcomed another Michigan giant."

MICKEY LOLICH AGAIN: "Al was the best player I ever saw and was picture perfect. He wasn't a rah-rah guy in the locker room but was the team leader by example. He hit in the clutch, ran well and was an outstanding fielder with a dead accurate arm."

BOB SEGER, ROCK & ROLL HALL OF FAME INDUCTEE FROM DETROIT: "He was a genuine hero of mine. I told him he and Willie Mays were my two favorite players of all-time and he sent me a photo of him and Willie, which I treasure."

JOE SCHMIDT, HALL OF FAME LINEBACKER FOR THE DETROIT LIONS: "He was always a fine gentleman. ... He never seemed liked he aged and was always in good shape."

CHRISTOPHER ILITCH, TIGERS OWNER: "Baseball lost a titan. ... Anyone who knew Al Kaline would describe his gentle soul and passion for baseball as an unbelievably powerful combination, making him one of the most respected players in Major League Baseball history. My mother, father and I cherished the special relationship we had with Al Kaline, who was a trusted advisor and dear friend for

CONTINUED ON PAGE 63

Willie and Al

JULIAN H. GONZALEZ

At the 2005 All-Star Game in Comerica Park, Willie Horton and Al Kaline threw out ceremonial first pitches. Each reached the plate. Fox, though, did not show them and cut off Ernie Harwell talking about Kaline in a pregame interview.

Willie Horton met Al Kaline as a youngster, 10 or 11 years old, in the weeks after slipping into Briggs Stadium with a couple of buddies after playing "strikeout" against one of the walls.

"It's my whole life," Horton said of a picture sent to him, showing him flanked by Kaline and Jake Wood. "I look at those three people and that's all of Willie Horton's life as a professional. I became a strong man, learned how to carry myself in the community and be a better person. (Kaline) was the kind of guy that set an example for all of us."

Horton grew up idolizing Kaline on the ballfields of Detroit and then played with him on the Tigers' 1968 championship team.

"I looked up to him as a young man, not as a ballplayer," Horton said. "But I looked at him as a hero and a father figure. He kind of showed me and the rest of guys how to become a professional athlete — that what you do off the field was just as important as what you do on the field. ... I still don't have the words ... to express my love to him and his family."

– Anthony Fenech

CONTINUED FROM PAGE 62
many years."

JIM PALMER, HALL OF FAME PITCHER FOR THE BALTIMORE ORIOLES: "One of my favorite people, Al Kaline, passed away. Such a graceful, elegant player. Always put the Tigers on my away schedule, just to see, talk with Al."

MATT SHEPARD, TIGERS BROADCASTER: "Always took time to share a smile and story over the years I've known him."

FRANK TANANA, DETROIT-BORN PITCHER FOR SIX TEAMS OVER 21 YEARS, INCLUDING THE TIGERS FROM 1985-92: "Al Kaline was one of my boyhood heroes along with Sandy Koufax. My dad, who had played minor-league ball, told me that I had to play the game like Kaline because he was so fundamentally sound. It was my delight to pitch against him."

DANIEL NORRIS, TIGERS PITCHER: "He garnered respect that he never assumed. His love and his compassion were staples in the Tiger clubhouse. ... He taught us about baseball but more importantly taught us how to be better men."

MARK SNYDER, FORMER DETROIT FREE PRESS SPORTSWRITER: "As sincere as any star athlete. He always had time, stopped to chat and offer insight. Having Al and Ernie was an abundance of riches for every young sports reporter in our city, welcoming with no pretense."

JOHN HICKS, FORMER TIGERS CATCHER AND FIRST BASEMAN: "Will always remember him walking by my locker and putting me in a headlock every day."

SEAN CASEY, FORMER TIGERS FIRST BASEMAN: "Al was so humble and kind to me when I got traded to Detroit in 2006. When we went to the World

CONTINUED ON PAGE 64

CONTINUED FROM PAGE 63

Series, his excitement for all of us felt like he was still playing. Kindest person ever, and one of the greatest to ever lace up the spikes!"

GRETCHEN WHITMER, MICHIGAN GOVERNOR: "He was a legend on and off the field. Through his 22 seasons with the team, he brought joy to generations of Tigers fans across our state as he worked his way into the 3,000 club."

MICKEY LOLICH AGAIN: "He never dropped the ball. If he ever got an error it was likely because he threw to third and the ball was so accurate it hit the runner."

ROCKY COLAVITO, TIGERS TEAMMATE, 1960-63: "Al was a super athlete, a superstar. He could to everything. He could run, field, throw, hit and hit with power. He was just a really good guy and a great teammate."

TONY KUBEK, FORMER NEW YORK YANKEE AND NBC BROADCASTER: "He wasn't the greatest player I played against, but he was probably the most perfect of all of them in understanding how to play the game. It was the way he ran the bases, fielded and hit. He was the ideal player and had an endearing love of the game."

DENNY MCCLAIN AGAIN: "He was the one to convince me to pitch in the sixth game of the '68 World Series. My arm was killing me. He said, 'You're going to pitch, right? We got nobody else, you're it, you've done it all year, just do it one more time.' That's all I had to hear."

NICHOLAS CASTELLANOS, TIGERS OUTFIELDER WHO CHOSE UNIFORM NO. 6 AFTER HIS 2019 TRADE TO THE CUBS: "A role model. He's somebody who's the face of the Tigers. Just a stand-up gentleman and a phenomenal baseball player."

JUSTIN VERLAND-

JULIAN H. GONZALEZ

Al Kaline, going old school without protective googles, and Justin Verlander doused each other with champagne as the Tigers celebrated an AL Central title in October 2012, their second of four straight division crowns.

ER, FORMER TIGERS PITCHER: "Such a kind and generous man who meant so much to so many. I hope you knew how much I enjoyed our conversations about baseball, life or just giving each other a hard time. I am honored to have been able to call you my friend for all these years."

BUCK FARMER, TIGERS PITCHER: "One of the best days in my short MLB career was being able to sit down in a Baltimore restaurant and share a cup of coffee with not only an incredible baseball player but an even better human being."

GRAYSON GREINER, TIGERS CATCHER: "Your stories and advice brought a smile to everybody's face on a daily basis."

JERRY GREEN, DETROIT NEWS COLUMNIST: "The first ball game I ever covered, the Tigers were playing the White Sox. Kaline hit a homer to right in the fourth inning. Then, it started to rain. They never finished the game, so it wasn't official. With that one, he would've hit 400. I told him that story many years later, and Al said, 'I don't remember it.' I said, 'I do!' and had the clipping to show him — one paragraph for the Associated Press."

REGGIE JACKSON AGAIN: "I would see him at the Hall of Fame and it was a badge of honor for me because he was always so nice to me. I saw him at spring training a couple of months ago and we hugged. I knew it was going to be the last time I saw him and it broke my heart. I could see he was leaving. He was such a genuine, graceful and beautiful human being."

ROB MANFRED, BASEBALL COMMISSIONER: "Many of us who are fortunate enough to work in baseball have our short lists of players who mean the most to us. Al Kaline was one of those players for me and countless others."

BARRY SANDERS, HALL OF FAME RUNNING BACK FOR THE DETROIT LIONS: "It is always devastating to lose someone

CONTINUED ON PAGE 65

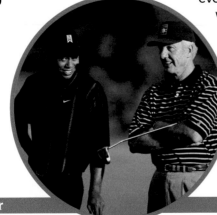

"You can tell he can really play ... even though he's got a little bit of a bad back," Tiger Woods said of partner Al Kaline, an eight handicapper at 68, after the 2003 Buick Open pro-am.
JULIAN H. GONZALEZ

'All you could see was the 6'

JULIAN
H. GONZALEZ

Jeff Daniels is a Michigander and one of the country's most recognizable and accomplished actors. He's also a lifelong Tigers fan who idolized Al Kaline growing up.

Al Kaline was the only player I ever saw who could make the ball come to him.

With the runner rounding second, he'd sprint into the rightfield corner and in one graceful motion the ball would find his glove. When he turned his back, all you could see was the 6. And when he threw the ball it would leave his hand like an air rocket, dead straight, screaming over the infield all the way in to the third-base bag. Don Wert never had to move his glove. The runner, of course, would be out by a mile.

That's how you remember childhood heroes.

Al Kaline was mine.

I still have the small wooden bat from 1964 Tigers bat day with his name on it.

I always will.

CONTINUED FROM PAGE 64
who means so much to the city."

FRANK TANANA AGAIN: "When I retired, we were members together at Oakland Hills Country Club and became dear friends. He was amazingly humble and always so nice to me."

ROD ALLEN, FORMER TIGERS BROADCASTER: "He was one the classiest men I've ever met. Always willing to share his baseball knowledge."

TONY KUBEK AGAIN: "I'll never forget one of his at-bats in the 1968 World Series against Bob Gibson when he kept fouling off pitch after pitch. He finally lined a single to center. Gibson walked a little towards first base and nodded at Al. He was giving him his due, like, 'You won that one, Al.' Coming from Bob Gibson, that meant a lot."

AL AVILA, TIGERS GENERAL MANAGER: "I was blessed to sit next to him during nearly every home game at Comerica Park, and I hold close our bond that has been created over nearly two decades of working together."

NICHOLAS CASTELLANOS AGAIN: "He was just the epitome of 'stay the course.' Through the whole rebuild thing, he was a big reason why I wanted to stay. Because he played (many) years with the Tigers before they made the postseason. Just hearing the stories of where he was at when they started just taught me patience more than anything."

JERRY LEWIS, DIRECTOR, TIGERS FANTASY CAMP: "Before Jim Price and I started the fantasy camp in 1984, Jim called Al about the idea and he loved it. It was the incentive for Jim to call the other '68 Tigers and they all joined in when Al said he would do it. He was terrific with all the campers and always participated. His No. 6 has always been the most popular number at the camp."

SPENCER TURNBULL, TIGERS PITCHER: "You're one of the wisest and kindest men I've met, and you always took a genuine interest in others. Your presence will not be forgotten."

PEDRO GOMEZ, ESPN REPORTER: "I have very rarely asked for a photograph with anyone, but several years ago I made an exception for my childhood favorite player. Such a gentle and giving man."

RAY LANE, FORMER TIGERS BROADCAST-ER: "Al was a real gentleman. He was quiet in the clubhouse, quiet on the field, but he was noisy with the bat. He was such a superb fielder. Among his friends, he also had a good sense of humor. He was just a good guy."

DICK VITALE, ESPN BROADCASTER WHO COACHED U-D AND THE PISTONS: "Breaks my heart. ... As a baseball lover, I was lucky to get to know Al during my time in the Detroit area."

ALEX WILSON, TIGERS PITCHER: "I was so very lucky to have the conversations we had!"

FRANK TANANA AGAIN: "Towards the end of his life he began to come to Bible studies and chapel on Sundays at the ballpark, and he came to know the Lord."

DENNY MCCLAIN AGAIN: "When I had my personal troubles, Al was still with me 100%. He never got off the bus like some others. He never took a cheap shot. He said he would never say anything against me because your wife loves you and you have four great kids."

ALAN TRAMMELL AGAIN: "I knew his health had deteriorated, but you always thought Al would live forever."

Six, by No. 6

A once-in-a-lifetime throw.
An inning that will last forever. A title.
One more grasp at team glory. A milestone
hit. And, at last, a date with baseball
immortality. Here are the epic moments
that defined 22 seasons in Detroit.

Before the 1962 season, his 10th in the big leagues, Al Kaline revealed: "I really have two ambitions now. Besides playing in the World Series, I'd like to play in the majors for 20 years." He exceeded the latter goal by two seasons.
MALCOLM EMMONS

Still learning to hit in the big leagues, Mr. Tiger was already a teenage dream as an outfielder

Nailed 'em again!

BY GENE MYERS

In three straight innings, once upon a time, from his lair in rightfield, Al Kaline actually nailed a Chicago White Sox runner trying for an extra base.

By July 7, 1954 — halfway through his first full season with the Tigers — Kaline had established himself as a top-shelf fielder. Even manager Fred Hutchison had gushed: "Kaline keeps making the kinds of plays we haven't seen in rightfield in years."

Then came a nondescript game in another nondescript season typical of the Tigers in the 1950s. They already were 20½ games out of first place — and 14½ behind that day's opponent at Briggs Stadium, the third-place Chicago White Sox. Only 5,099 fans bothered to come to The Corner on a summer Wednesday afternoon.

After 2 hours, 28 minutes, the speedy White Sox had coasted to a 9-0 victory behind 16 hits. But the talk of the day became the arm of the Tigers' skinny and shy 19-year-old rightfielder. This game, his 99th in the big leagues, did more than any prior to brandish his defensive reputation and serve as a precursor to his 10 Gold Gloves and 22-season Hall of Fame career.

The Detroit Free Press wrote: "Only some spectacular fielding by Al Kaline kept the count from going higher. ... Kaline now has pegged out five runners at home this season and retired two others at third."

The Detroit Times wrote: "Al Kaline has again proved that rivals are not to take liberties with his remarkable arm without courting danger."

The Detroit News wrote: "Gratitude for the work of Al Kaline was about

CONTINUED ON PAGE 70

Because he hardly played in 1953, Al Kaline's rookie season officially was 1954. His superior defense helped him finish third in the rookie of the year balloting. That year's runners-up included three future Hall of Famers: Kaline in the AL, Ernie Banks and Henry Aaron in the NL.
DETROIT FREE PRESS

CONTINUED FROM PAGE 68

all the Tigers could muster to relieve the gloom of the clubhouse after their annihilation by the White Sox. ... In successive innings three runners were cut down by the arm of the Baltimore bonus player as they attempted to deepen Detroit's humiliation."

In the second inning, the White Sox took a 2-0 lead off left-hander Billy Hoeft on Fred Marsh's one-out double. After a walk and a lineout, Nellie Fox drilled a single to rightfield. Kaline fired a strike to catcher Frank House; the throw beat Marsh by so much that House had plenty of time to block the plate and to brace himself for a collision. Marsh lowered a shoulder, House and Marsh crashed to the ground, but House held on to the ball, ending the inning and giving Kaline his first assist of the game.

In the third inning, Hoeft's day ended with a pair of leadoff singles to leftfield by Minnie Minoso and Ron Jackson. After Ray Herbert walked Sherm Lollar to load the bases, Jim Rivera singled off second baseman Frank Bolling's glove to score two runs. That left runners at the corners for Johnny Groth, who singled to Kaline. As Lollar coasted home from third, Rivera, who would steal 18 bases in '54, raced to go from first to third. Kaline fired another strike, this time to third baseman Ray Boone. Kaline's throw beat Rivera by more than five feet, and all Boone had to do was tag Rivera when he eventually arrived via a headfirst slide.

In the fourth inning, the White Sox built their lead to 5-0 on a single by Chico Carrasquel and a double by Fox. Minoso made it 6-0 with a long drive to right. But Minoso, who led the league with 25 steals in '53, wasn't content stopping at second and Kaline made him pay. He fired the ball to Bolling and Minoso was stuck in no-man's land. A rundown ensued: Bolling to shortstop Harvey Kuenn to Boone to Kuenn.

Kuenn's tag of Minoso not that far from second base gave Kaline his

third outfield assist of the game and an assist in three straight innings.

Kaline fell one assist shy of the American League record, set by Ducky Holmes of the Chicago White Stockings in 1903 and equaled four times, but not since 1928.

None of Detroit's three daily newspapers quoted Kaline in their reports the next day. Such coverage would be unlikely these days but was common at the time.

In "The Al Kaline Story," a 1964 biography, Al Hirshberg, a prolific freelance writer from Boston, wrote: "When Al was congratulated in the locker room for the almost unbelievable feat of throwing three men out from rightfield, he could do nothing

CONTINUED ON PAGE 73

Bottoms up! Kaline nails runner from his fanny

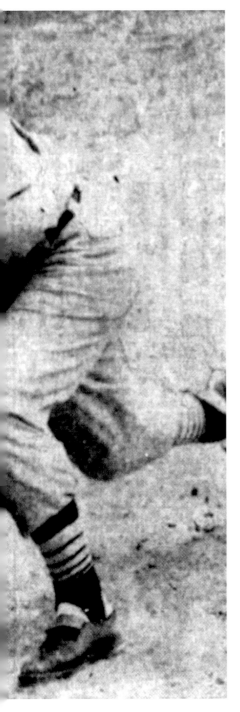

Right from the start of his career, Al Kaline made remarkable catches in the outfield and nailed baserunners who dared to test his arm. When he threw out a Chicago White Sox baserunner in three consecutive innings in July 1954, only 5,099 fans were in the green seats of Briggs Stadium. For his next career-defining defensive feat, five weeks later, 53,778 fans were packed into Briggs Stadium.

On Aug. 10, 1954, a Tuesday night, the downtrodden Tigers were playing the first-place Cleveland Indians — owners of baseball's best record at 76-32 (.703). The Tigers' Ned Garver fired a five-hit shutout, 4-0. He walked no one and did not allow an extra-base hit. But the talk of the summer night was a catch that Kaline failed to make.

Free Press sports editor Lyall Smith filed this report:

"Ned was protecting a one-run lead given him by Wayne Belardi's 11th homer in the fourth inning when he ran into a jam in the Indians' eighth. With one out and the Tribe smarting under a two-hit diet, pinch-hitter Dale Mitchell dropped a single into rightfield.

"Kaline dove for the ball, fell down and missed it. He reached behind him, picked it up and then — still sitting down — threw his strike to second base in time to catch Mitchell.

"The next two batters came through with singles, but they meant nothing because of Kaline's pitch."

Three biographies about Kaline — written in 1964, 1973 and 2010 — provided slightly different ac-

DETROIT FREE PRESS

When Chicago's Fred Marsh, leading with his shoulder while running at full tilt, failed to jar the ball loose from Frank House in the second inning, Al Kaline had his first assist on July 7, 1954. The Free Press declared Marsh used "football tactics."

DETROIT FREE PRESS

While Al Kaline got it done from his butt on Aug. 10, 1954, Wayne Belardi got it done with his bat. He smiled as he crossed the plate after a fourth-inning solo home run.

counts of his signature throw. One said his throw from shallow right to shortstop Harvey Kuenn had "the speed of a bullet." Two said Mitchell returned to the dugout shaking his head and muttering, "My god, what an arm that kid has."

– Gene Myers

The day when Mr. Tiger robbed the Mick

Kaline's Circus Catch Saves Sweep of Yanks

— Detroit Free Press headline

Kaline's Catch Ranks With Greatest

— Detroit Times headline

Al Kaline's most famous catch came in Yankee Stadium in the 1950s — when against the fence, running and leaping at full speed, he robbed Mickey Mantle of a two-out, bottom-of-the-ninth, walk-off blast.

Kaline's catch produced two interesting backstories — what happened in right-center and what happened in the clubhouse — plus capped a doubleheader sweep of the first-place Yankees.

Hal Middlesworth of the Free Press described the action on the field on July 18, 1956: "You would have to see it to believe it — the thrilling catch Al Kaline made. ... It was one of those once-in-a-lifetime grabs for the young outfielder, a breathtaking finish to an exciting afternoon. ...

"Kaline loomed up out of rightfield and reached the bleacher scoreboard just as the ball sailed overhead. With a prodigious spring, he leaped almost to the top of the wire fence atop the wall, stuck up his gloved hand and came down with the ball."

In the Tigers' clubhouse, a letter carrier named Mickey Rendine, who doubled as the visiting attendant, was laying out towels and listening to the radio. Mantle's blast was hit so hard that a Yankees broadcaster — it's uncertain whether it was the legendary Mel Allen or his assistant, Jim Woods — quickly called it a home run and a New York victory. Rendine switched off the radio and prepared for a collection of glum-faced Tigers.

Instead, Joe Falls wrote for the Detroit Times, "suddenly, almost violently, the door crashed open and the Tigers streamed in, yelling, singing and dancing." Rendine couldn't believe it. The Detroit News quoted Rendine as telling the team, "I thought you guys blew it."

"Man, didn't you see it!" Falls quoted an unnamed player telling Rendine. "What a catch! Kaline took the ball right out of the sky."

The News quoted Rendine again: "I expected to see a lot of sad-looking guys come in here, and I couldn't understand why you were laughing and skylarking."

Falls wrote that "the least excited of all the players was Kaline." He certainly wasn't skylarking, which, for the record, includes inducing horseplay and frolicking among its definitions.

"It wasn't such a hard catch," Kaline said. "I thought it would be a homer, too, at first, but then I thought I'd have a chance for it.

"I just had to time my leap right, that's all."

Falls noted that "Kaline didn't complain about it, but there was an ugly purple-red mark across his back where he slammed against the scoreboard."

– Gene Myers

Al Kaline's big-league career got a jumpstart in spring 1954 when Steve (Bud) Souchock, a journeyman the Tigers were counting on to be the rightfielder, suffered a broken wrist playing winter ball in Cuba. Kaline was thrown into the starting lineup at 19 years old and stayed there for more than two decades.
DETROIT FREE PRESS

CONTINUED FROM PAGE 70

but grin. And when a newspaperman asked him how he felt about it, he stammered, 'That was a fair day. I liked it.'

"So did the Tigers and their fans. On that one day, Kaline stamped himself as a baseball star and a hometown favorite. The word spread quickly around the league, and from then on, opposing ballplayers ran the bases with great care whenever the ball was hit to him.

"Hutch, of course, was delighted. 'When he does things like that,' he enthused, 'I don't care if he hits .200.'"

In "Al Kaline and the Detroit Tigers," a 1973 biography, Hal Butler, a prolific jack-of-all-trades writer and editor from Detroit, wrote: "Kaline's three assists ... assured him that very few runners would henceforth take a chance on his throwing arm. Al, in his modest way, acknowledged the feat to reporters merely by saying, 'That was a fair day. Real fair. I liked it.'"

The Tigers never planned on using Kaline as their everyday rightfielder in 1954. The job belonged to Steve (Bud) Souchock, who would have started the season as a 35-year-old who had never reached 300 at-bats in a season. But Souchock had hit .302 with 11 home runs in 89 games in 1953, which, for that Tigers era, wasn't half bad.

Souchock, though, suffered a broken wrist playing winter ball in Cuba. In equal parts admiration and desperation, Hutchinson announced that Kaline, less than nine months after graduating from high school, would take Souchock's place during Grapefruit League games but Souchock would be the starter when

his wrist healed, with luck in time for Opening Day.

In the 1950s, when there wasn't an entry draft, baseball tried to prevent bidding wars for amateur players with this hammer: Anyone signed for more than $4,000 had to spend two years in the majors before he could be sent to the minors for seasoning.

Kaline had signed for $35,000, according to the team, in June 1953. Like most "bonus babies" at the time, he rarely saw the field. In three-plus months with the Tigers, he played in only 30 games and came to the plate only 30 times. In nine games, all he did was pinch run. He might see the field in the late innings of the blowout or when Hutchinson ran out of bodies. Until his first start, on Sept. 16, 1953, when he went 3-for-5, Kaline had never played before the fifth inning and had played before the seventh inning only four times.

He finished with a .250 average (7-for-28) with a home run (his only extra-base hit) and two runs batted in (both in September). He scored nine runs — five as a pinch runner. He walked once, was hit by a pitch and struck out five times.

At Lakeland, Florida, in 1954, for his first spring training, Kaline caught fire. That prompted the Free Press' sports editor, Lyall Smith, to file this report in late March: "Kaline, the slender but slick bonus baby from Baltimore, is the hottest item on a squad. ...

"Al has been used in all three outfield spots. Only twice has he started, and finished, a game. Hutchinson prefers to use him for 'spot' duty.

"But the way he is performing will make it practically impossible for Hutchinson to keep him out of his

CONTINUED ON PAGE 74

CONTINUED FROM PAGE 73

outfield. Kaline has slapped out nine hits in 16 tries for a sparkling .563 average.

"One of those blows was a long home run. Another was a triple. A third one was a double.

"He is the fastest man in camp. He is an excellent fielder. His throwing arm is strong. Despite his age, his baseball savvy is sound."

When Souchock's injury continued to linger, Hutchinson told Kaline in Florida: "You're my rightfielder until somebody else shows me they can take the job away from you."

Plenty of people — in the front office, dugout, press box and stands — wondered whether Kaline could hit enough to play in the majors. Kaline admitted in a 1964 interview with Sports Illustrated that he wondered, too.

"I was there because I was a fielder," Kaline told the magazine's Jack Olsen. "That's what kept me in the league. The question was: Did I have enough bat?"

He was hitting under .200 in late April. He bumped his average by nearly 100 points at times in May but finished the month with only two extra-base hits. In June, he belted a grand slam against the Philadelphia Athletics — at 19, the second youngest to do so in baseball history — but contributed only three RBIs for the rest of the month. In July, he didn't have an extra-base hit until July 18 and finished the month batting .247 for the season.

On July 7, the day he threw out the three White Sox, Kaline singled in three at-bats, raising his average to .251.

Kaline's bat heated up in August: He went 37-for-89 (.416) with 10 extra-base hits and 10 RBIs. But he struggled again in September: 20-for-83 (.241) with two doubles.

Kaline finished his first full season hitting a respectable .276 (139-for-504) but with only 25 extra-base hits and 43 RBIs over 138 games. He fin-

JULIAN H. GONZALEZ

The man with the Gold Glove (10 of 'em actually), Al Kaline never shied away from discussing leather and glove work with a youngster such as Gene Kingsale, a 26-year-old outfielder from Aruba who played 39 games for the Tigers in 2003.

ished third in the rookie of the year balloting, though, behind Yankees right-hander Bob Grim (20-6, 3.26 ERA) and A's third baseman Jim Finigan (.302, seven homers, 51 RBIs).

(The National League rookie of the year was Cardinals centerfielder Wally Moon. The NL runners-up featured two future Hall of Famers: Cubs shortstop Ernie Banks and Braves leftfielder Henry Aaron. All first-ballot inductees, Banks made Cooperstown in 1977, Kaline in 1980 and Aaron in 1982.)

For much of Kaline's rookie season, it certainly was his glove that kept

him in the lineup. His three-assist game was the highlight of highlights. But a month later he delivered another signature defensive moment that would be referenced for the rest of his career: He threw out a runner while sitting on his bottom in the outfield grass.

By the end of the next season, Kaline had married his high school sweetheart, gained 20 pounds, belted three home runs in a game, started in the All-Star Game, and erased Ty Cobb from the record book as the youngest player to win a batting championship.

Kaline's Golden (Glove) years

Started in 1957, the Gold Glove Award honors the best defenders at each position in the American League and in the National League. Tigers rightfielder Al Kaline won 10 Gold Gloves — a figure that certainly would have been higher if the award had started with his rookie season of 1954. He shares the record for Gold Gloves by an AL outfielder with Ken Griffey Jr. and Ichiro Suzuki.

In 1957, separate Gold Gloves were not awarded in the AL and NL. That year, Kaline won the Gold Glove as the rightfielder, Minnie Minoso of the Chicago White Sox as the left-fielder and Willie Mays of the New York Giants as the centerfielder.

Kaline then won a Gold Glove each year through 1967 except for 1960. In 1958, Kaline won as a rightfielder. In 1959, Kaline won as a centerfield-er (he played 121 games in center, 15 in right). In 1960, Kaline played 142 games in the field, all at center; however, the Gold Glove for center-field went to Jim Landis of the White Sox.

From 1961-2010, Gold Gloves were awarded to the top three outfield-ers, regardless of position. Starting in 1961, Kaline played the majority of his games in rightfield the rest of the decade, although he played in center 22 times in 1961 and more in center than right in 1965 (62 games vs. 51) and 1966 (86 games vs. 54). In 1967, when he won his 10th and final Gold Glove, he spent 130 games in right-field and one inning in centerfield.

In 1968, an early season broken forearm and the emergence of Jim Northrup limited Kaline to 70 games in rightfield. He also spent parts of five games in leftfield and 22 games, including 18 starts, at first base. The Gold Glovers that year were Detroit's Mickey Stanley, Boston's Carl Yas-trzemski and Boston's Reggie Smith.

In 1972 and '73, Kaline played right-field and first base. In 1974, the last of his 22 seasons, he never played in the field. To stay healthy at age 39 for his successful pursuit of 3,000 hits, he served as a full-time desig-nated hitter.

Only Roberto Clemente and Mays, each with 12, have more outfield Gold Gloves than Kaline, Griffey and Suzuki.

Like Kaline, if the award had started sooner, Mays, a rookie in 1951, likely would have won three more times (and possibly a fourth). Mays won a Gold Glove every year from 1957-68, his last at age 37.

Clemente, a rookie in 1955, did not win his first Gold Glove until 1961. His streak of 12 straight, the last at age 38 in 1972, ended with his tragic death Dec. 31, 1972, when his plane crashed in the sea while deliver-ing supplies from his homeland of Puerto Rico to earthquake victims in Nicaragua.

From 1957-67, while Kaline was winning 10 Gold Gloves, the other AL outfielders with multiple Gold Gloves were Landis (five), Minoso (three), Yastrzemski (three) and Jimmy Pier-sall (two).

— Gene Myers

Outfields of dreams

A list of Al Kaline's Gold Glove awards — and the other outfield recipients in those years:

YEAR	POS	KALINE'S GAMES	OTHER OF WINNERS
1957	RF	RF 136, CF 23, LF 5	Minnie Minoso, CWS; Willie Mays NYG
1958	RF	RF 142, CF 4	Norm Siebern, NYY; Jimmy Piersall, BOS
1959	CF	CF 121, RF 15	Minnie Minoso, CWS; Jackie Jensen, BOS
1961	OF	RF 141, CF 22, LF 1	Jim Landis, CWS; Jimmy Piersall, CLE
1962	OF	RF 100	Jim Landis, CWS; Mickey Mantle, NYY
1963	OF	RF 139, CF 2	Jim Landis, CWS; Carl Yastrzemski, BOS
1964	OF	RF 136	Jim Landis, CWS; Vic Davalillo, CLE
1965	OF	CF 62, RF 51	Carl Yastrzemski, BOS; Tom Tresh, NYY
1966	OF	CF 86, RF 64	Tommie Agee, CWS; Tony Oliva, MIN
1967	OF	RF 130, CF 1	Carl Yastrzemski, BOS; Paul Blair, BAL

DETROIT FREE PRESS

In the 1960s, Carl Yastrzemski's name often appeared with Al Kaline's near the top of the batting statistics and in the Gold Glove honor roll.

With three mighty swings in one April 1955 game, Kaline staked a claim as one of the AL's top hitters

Three's company

BY GENE MYERS

Move over, you immortals of baseball! Make room in the record book for Al Kaline!

The Tigers' slender 20-year-old outfielder — not yet two years out of high school — made his big bid for lasting fame Sunday before 16,662 fans at Briggs Stadium.

He smashed out three home runs, two in one inning, as the Bengals swamped the Kansas City Athletics, 16 to 0. ...

Even against the Athletics' minor-league-grade pitching, Kaline's performance was a tremendous feat.

With those words, Hal Middlesworth of the Free Press gushed about the most unexpected day of slugging in Tigers history.

Even though Kaline by the late 1960s would be the Tigers' career leader in homers — a mark he still holds with 399, even though he never considered himself a home-run hitter — at the start of the 1955 season he not only wasn't a power hitter, the question hovered over this superlative-fielding young outfielder whether he could hit with enough oomph even to stay in the major leagues.

As a seldom-used bonus baby in 1953, Kaline had hit one home run. As the starting rightfielder in 1954, despite 504 at-bats, he had hit only four home runs. In fact, in 1954, he managed only 25 hits for extra bases out of 139, a mere .347 slugging percentage.

After April 17, 1955, against the Athletics, the Tigers' sixth game of the season, Kaline not only had 14 hits in 25 at-bats, but nearly half his hits had gone for extra bases — three homers, two triples and a double. Plus, he had knocked in 12 runs.

The remarkable math: In 138 games in 1954, Kaline had 25 hits for extra bases. In six games in 1955, Kaline had six hits for extra bases. His sudden power dumbfounded the media, his teammates, his coaches — and himself.

"That's something, isn't it?" he said after his three-homer game. "My stance and swing are the same. And I'm using the same bat."

"Shy Guy with Big Bat" declared the headline atop the front page of the Free Press.

The Free Press noted that Kaline had added 20 pounds since the 1954 season, from 155 to 175, "but on his 6-foot-1 frame, it doesn't show." The Free Press also noted that Kaline, still painfully shy eight months from his 21st birthday, had married his high school sweetheart, Louise Hamilton, during the off-season, implying that her cooking was doing the job of fattening him up. Asked in the locker room whether his bride, indeed, was a good cook, Kaline replied: "She is."

Middlesworth wrote: "No one could have picked Kaline as the newest addition to baseball's honor roll of slugging. Not until someone mentioned that his name will go into the record book did the 20-year-old bonus baby muster a weak smile. ...

"Otherwise, the slender youth, who stepped off the campus of Baltimore's Southern High School in June

CONTINUED ON PAGE 80

On June 23, 1953, Al Kaline met the Tigers in Philadelphia and donned an old English D for the first time. The Free Press wrote: "Kaline, a quiet, almost frail-looking youngster, took a short batting practice with the Tigers, then shagged flies until the game started. He had trouble with pitcher Hal Erickson's tosses, getting only one ball out of the infield." Manager Fred Hutchinson insisted it was too early to pass judgment on Kaline's batting skills and then noted: "Looks like he has a good pair of hands." Kaline made his big-league debut two days later.
ASSOCIATED PRESS

Nobody did it younger than Kaline, even Cobb

In 1955, in his second full season, still strikingly skinny and terminally shy, Al Kaline coasted to the American League batting championship with a .340 average.

He hit safely in 25 of the season's first 26 games and 31 of its first 33. He batted .429 in April. No player other than Kaline collected 200 hits. The batting race really never was a race at all: Kaline finished 21 points ahead of the runner-up, Kansas City's Vic Power.

On Sept. 26, 1955, the morning after the season finale for the fifth-place Tigers and the opener for the Detroit Lions — winners of three straight division titles — the main photograph on the Sports section of the Free Press featured a pair of casually dressed 20-year-old newlyweds, Al and Louise Kaline. The caption read: "Batting title safely tucked away, Al Kaline and his wife, Louise, stroll toward the exit at Briggs Stadium. Al carries his favorite bats with him as he heads for home with a .340 average."

Still, Kaline's historic title was such a foregone conclusion that it warranted only a small, shared headline on the page: "Kaline and Boone Take AL Crowns." Yet, it became the official moment that haunted Kaline the rest of his career. It caused him in the 1960s to tell Sports Illustrated: "The worst thing that happened to me in the big leagues was the start I had. This put the pressure on me."

But in 1955 Kaline didn't feel that pressure. He was an unknown doing the unthinkable. And the man he edged to become baseball's youngest batting champion: Tigers legend Ty Cobb.

Throughout the decades, including the day after the 1955 season, reports of Kaline's batting title at age 20 inevitably said that he was one day younger than Cobb was when he won his title in 1907. Although Cobb's birth date was Dec. 18 and Kaline's was Dec. 19, Kaline actually was 12 days younger at the time of his title. Kaline won his on Sept. 25, 1955, at 20 years and 280 days. Cobb won his first on Oct. 6, 1907, at 20 years and 292 days.

Cobb, of course, didn't stop at one batting crown. He won nine straight titles — 1907-15 — lost to Cleveland's Tris Speaker despite batting .370 in 1916, and then won three more titles in a row — 1917-19.

Kaline never won another batting title, although he was a runner-up three times and third twice. The fans expected more titles. The press expected more titles. He even expected more titles. Frequently, Kaline became depressed, despite consistent, all-star caliber play.

"I was lucky that year," Kaline would tell people, year after year. "Everything fell into place."

After the '55 finale, Tigers president Spike Briggs staged a champagne party in the clubhouse. To celebrate the Tigers' most victories (79) and highest attendance (1,181,828) since 1950, third baseman Ray Boone sharing the RBI title with Boston's Jackie Jensen and the baby-faced outfield winning the 20th batting title in club history (13 more than the runner-up Indians).

"Everything I did was right that year," Kaline said decades later about the magic of '55. "For a long time, the pitchers didn't think I was for real. By the time they found out, the season was over and I had the batting championship."

— **Gene Myers**

Hit kings

Al Kaline was the sixth Tiger to lead the American League in batting average. The Tigers' champs:

PLAYER	YEAR	AVG	RUNNER-UP
Ty Cobb	1907	.350	Sam Crawford, Detroit, .323
Ty Cobb	1908	.324	Sam Crawford, Detroit, .311
Ty Cobb	1909	.377	Eddie Collins, Philadelphia, .347
Ty Cobb	1910	.385	Nap Lajoie, Cleveland, .384
Ty Cobb	1911	.419	Shoeless Joe Jackson, Cleveland, .408
Ty Cobb	1912	.409	Shoeless Joe Jackson, Cleveland, .395
Ty Cobb	1913	.389	Shoeless Joe Jackson, Cleveland, .373
Ty Cobb	1914	.368	Eddie Collins, Philadelphia, .344
Ty Cobb	1915	.369	Eddie Collins, Philadelphia, .332
Ty Cobb	1917	.383	George Sisler, St. Louis, .353
Ty Cobb	1918	.382	George Burns, Philadelphia, .352
Ty Cobb	1919	.384	Bobby Veach, Detroit, .355
Harry Heilmann	1921	.394	Ty Cobb, Detroit, .389
Harry Heilmann	1923	.403	Babe Ruth, New York, .393
Harry Heilmann	1925	.393	Tris Speaker, Cleveland, .389
Heinie Manush	1926	.378	Babe Ruth, New York, .372
Harry Heilmann	1927	.398	Al Simmons, Philadelphia, .392
Charlie Gehringer	1937	.371	Lou Gehrig, New York, .351
George Kell	1949	.343	Ted Williams, Boston, .343
Al Kaline	1955	.340	Vic Power, Kansas City, .319
Harvey Kuenn	1959	.353	Al Kaline, Detroit, .327
Norm Cash	1961	.361	Al Kaline, Detroit, .324
Magglio Ordonez	2007	.363	Ichiro Suzuki, Seattle, .351
Miguel Cabrera	2011	.344	Adrian Gonzalez, Boston, .338
Miguel Cabrera	2012	.330	Mike Trout, Los Angeles, .326
Miguel Cabrera	2013	.348	Joe Mauer, Minnesota, .324
Miguel Cabrera	2015	.338	Xander Bogaerts, Boston, .320

The famed Georgia Peach, Ty Cobb won 12 batting titles with the Tigers. In 22 seasons in Detroit, he batted .368 with 3,900 hits and 869 steals. Al Kaline and Cobb, who died in 1961 at 74, met during spring training in the 1950s. "I had always heard what a fierce man Ty Cobb was," Kaline said. "But when I met him, he was very mild-mannered." Then Kaline added: "He told me, 'Always bear down, because there'll come a time when you won't be able to bear down,' meaning there'll come a time when you won't be able to play."
DETROIT FREE PRESS

Monthly leaders

A look at the leaders in the 1955 American League batting race, month-by-month:

APRIL 29

PLAYER	TEAM	STATS	AVG
Al Kaline	Detroit	24-for-53	.453
Bill Skowron	New York	23-for-51	.451
Vic Power	Kansas City	22-for-54	.407
Faye Thorneberry	Boston	21-for-55	.382
Chico Carrasquel	Chicago	20-for-53	.377

JUNE 3

Harvey Kuenn	Detroit	59-for-155	.381
Al Kaline	Detroit	67-for-178	.376
Vic Power	Kansas City	49-for-145	.338
Sherm Lollar	Chicago	36-for-116	.310
Mickey Mantle	New York	50-for-163	.307

JULY 1

Al Kaline	Detroit	104-for-284	.366
Nellie Fox	Chicago	96-for-288	.333
Al Smith	Cleveland	98-for-304	.322
Harvey Kuenn	Detroit	79-for-254	.311
Larry Doby	Cleveland	71-for-229	.310

AUG. 5

Al Kaline	Detroit	145-for-414	.350
Harvey Kuenn	Detroit	135-for-414	.326
Al Smith	Cleveland	136-for-432	.315
George Kell	Chicago	94-for-301	.312
Vic Power	Kansas City	127-for-410	.310

SEPT. 2

Al Kaline	Detroit	182-for-519	.351
Vic Power	Kansas City	164-for-517	.317
Harvey Kuenn	Detroit	162-for-527	.307
Al Smith	Cleveland	161-for-525	.307
George Kell	Chicago	111-for-362	.307

FINAL LEADERS

Al Kaline	Detroit	200-for-588	.340
Vic Power	Kansas City	190-for-596	.319
George Kell	Chicago	134-for-429	.312
Nellie Fox	Chicago	198-for-636	.311
Harvey Kuenn	Detroit	190-for-620	.306
Al Smith	Cleveland	186-for-607	.306

DETROIT FREE PRESS

On the day Al Kaline hit three homers, Kansas City's Vic Power went 0-for-3 at Briggs Stadium. Each player was in his second full season, although with a seven-year age difference. From Puerto Rico, Power was 27. At season's end, Kaline (at .340) and Power (at .319) ranked 1-2 in the batting race.

CONTINUED FROM PAGE 76

1953 to claim ... the Tigers' bonus cash, was almost noncommittal.

"If he was thrilled, he wasn't showing it. And that was entirely in keeping with his background with the Tigers. He is the Bengals' unrivaled 'deadpan.'"

Kaline became the 89th player with a three-homer game, according to the Baseball Almanac. (It had been done 113 times.) He became the fifth Tiger with a three-homer game and first since Pat Mullin in 1949. (The others were Ty Cobb in 1925, Pinky Higgins in 1940 and Rudy York in 1941. A footnote: Hall-of-Famer Dan Brouthers did it in 1886 for the Detroit Wolverines of the National League.)

Kaline became the 11th player (and first Tiger) in the AL or NL with two homers in one inning and the first to accomplish the feat since Sid Gordon of the New York Giants in 1949. (The last American Leaguer with a two-homer inning was Joe DiMaggio of the New York Yankees in 1936.)

Batting third, Kaline drew a two-out walk in the first inning off Johnny Gray, a right-hander for the Athletics, who had relocated from Philadelphia to Kansas City during the off-season.

In the third inning, Fred Hatfield reached on an infield single with two outs. Kaline then belted Gray's hanging curveball into the lower leftfield stands for a 2-0 lead.

In the fourth inning, Kaline came up with one

CONTINUED ON PAGE 81

Kaline in 1955: The months

MONTH	G	AB	R	H	2B	3B	HR	RBI	BB	SO	BA	OBP	SLG	OPS
April	15	56	15	24	2	2	5	14	11	2	.429	.515	.804	1.318
May	27	110	17	37	4	2	3	20	12	10	.336	.407	.491	.897
June	27	111	25	41	4	2	6	19	14	11	.369	.441	.604	1.045
July	32	124	34	39	5	0	9	24	19	15	.315	.404	.573	.977
August	30	113	17	38	5	1	2	14	16	10	.336	.420	.451	.871
September	21	74	13	21	4	1	2	11	10	9	.284	.372	.446	.818
TOTALS	**152**	**588**	**121**	**200**	**24**	**8**	**27**	**102**	**82**	**57**	**.340**	**.421**	**.546**	**.967**

The Tigers started playing at Michigan and Trumbull when the American League debuted in 1901. Their first home was wooden Bennett Park. A steel-and-concrete stadium, called Navin Field after owner Frank Navin, opened at the same site on April 20, 1912, the same day as Boston's Fenway Park. Navin Field became Briggs Stadium in 1938 and, finally, Tiger Stadium in 1961. This photo showed Briggs Stadium in the 1950s.
DETROIT FREE PRESS

CONTINUED FROM PAGE 80

out, the bases loaded and three runs in. He looped a single to rightfield off right-hander Charlie Bishop to score pitcher Steve Gromek for a 6-0 lead. Two flyouts followed.

With the Tigers up, 7-0, Kaline led off the sixth inning against Bob Spicer, a 30-year-old right-hander making his big-league debut. Kaline belted a fastball 400 feet on a line into the lower left-center seats.

The next seven Tigers reached on a hit, a walk or an error against Spicer and right-hander Lee Wheat, whose final big-league appearance would come six days later. Hatfield made the inning's first out, a grounder to the second baseman that nonetheless scored the Tigers' 14th run and moved Harvey Kuenn from second to third. Against Bob Trice, another right-hander, the third reliever of the inning and the man who broke the Athletics' color line in September 1953, Kaline came up for the sec-

ond time in the sixth. He promptly blasted a slider into the lower leftfield stands for a two-run homer and the 16-0 lead.

According to Hal Butler's 1973 book "Al Kaline and the Detroit Tigers," Kaline made a "memorable eight-word speech as he collapsed on the bench. 'Wake me up, somebody,' he said. 'I think I'm dreaming.' 'It's no dream, kid,' one of the veteran players remarked. 'You're awake out there.'"

CONTINUED ON PAGE 83

A start for the ages

Signing the morning after his high school graduation in June 1953, Tigers outfielder Al Kaline played in 30 games that season, usually in the late innings of blowouts. He made only four starts, all in centerfield, and came to the plate only 30 times. He finished at .250 (7-for-28) with one homer and six singles. His slash line: .250/.300/.357.

In 1954, officially his rookie season, Kaline started 133 games, all in rightfield. He played in 138. He came to the plate 535 times. He hit a respectable .276 (139-for-504) but managed only 25 hits for extra bases — four homers, three triples and 18 doubles — and 43 runs batted in. His first homer didn't come until June 11, a grand slam off Moe Burtschy of the Philadelphia Athletics. His slash line: .276/.305/.347.

In 1955, Kaline came out of the starting gate like Secretariat. His slash line after six games: .560/.571/1.120. He got a hit in the season's first 14 games, walked twice in an O-fer on April 30, got a hit in the next 11 games, suffered another O-fer on May 13 and got a hit in the next six games. After two singles and three RBIs on May 20, he had gotten a hit in 31 of the season's first 33 games with a slash line of .380/.460/.643. Kaline also finished the season like Secretariat, winning the batting title at age 20 by 21 points over Kansas City's Vic Power. A game-by-game look at his scorching start:

TUESDAY, APRIL 12, 1955, AT KANSAS CITY: A pair of singles in four at-bats. Athletics 6, Tigers 2.

WEDNESDAY, APRIL 13, AT KANSAS CITY: A double and a single in five at-bats, two RBIs, two runs. Tigers 10, Athletics 2.

THURSDAY, APRIL 14, AT DETROIT: Two triples in four at-bats, three RBIs. Indians 5, Tigers 3.

FRIDAY, APRIL 15, AT DETROIT: Two singles in four at-bats, an RBI on a sacrifice fly. Indians 7, Tigers 3.

SATURDAY, APRIL 16, AT DETROIT: Two singles in three at-bats, a walk and a run. Tigers 8, Athletics 3.

SUNDAY, APRIL 17, AT DETROIT: Three homers and a single in five at-bats, plus six RBIs, three runs, a walk and 13 total bases. Tigers 16, Athletics 0.

THURSDAY, APRIL 21, AT DETROIT: Solo homer in four at-bats. White Sox 9, Tigers 1.

TOTALS AFTER SEVEN GAMES: 15-for-29, eight singles, four homers, two triples, one double, 13 RBIs, seven runs, two walks and one sacrifice fly. Slash line — .517/.531/1.103. OPS — 1.635. Pace for 154 games — 330 hits, 154 runs, 88 homers, 286 RBIs.

— **Gene Myers**

After Al Kaline entered the lineup, the Tigers put their faith in (from the left) Kaline in right, Ray Boone at third, Bill Tuttle in center, Red Wilson at catcher and Fred Hatfield at second baseman. Most were discarded within a few years by the mediocre Tigers.
DETROIT FREE PRESS

CONTINUED FROM PAGE 81

Kaline came to bat again in the eighth inning with a chance to join the handful of sluggers with four homers in a game. Kuenn had led off with a double, his third of the game, and Hatfield had struck out. Alas, Trice retired Kaline on a pop to the shortstop.

Trice was by far the Athletics' top pitcher this day: He threw three innings and surrendered only one run. However, his days in the majors ended at age 28 after surrendering five runs on April 23 and six on May 2.

Kaline finished 4-for-5 with three homers, six RBIs, three runs, one single, one walk and 13 total bases.

"Quite a performance," manager Bucky Harris summarized. (Middlesworth wrote "no one was more tickled by Kaline's wrecking job" than the skipper.)

The Free Press wondered whether Kaline could "continue the staggering slugging" to start the season. "I'd like to have a couple more weeks like that," Kaline said with a grin.

Kaline, of course, couldn't keep up his 1.691 on-base-plus-slugging percentage. But he never stopped hitting in 1955. Or doing so with power. He became the youngest batting champion (hitting .340). Of his 200 hits, 59 went for extra bases (including 27 homers). He drove in 102 runs (59 more than in 1954). And he finished second in the MVP voting (behind Yogi Berra of the pennant-winning Yankees).

The hype surrounding Kaline's three-homer game continued for several days. The Tigers weren't scheduled to play again until Wednesday afternoon at home against the Chicago White Sox. Harris scheduled a six-inning intrasquad game for Monday afternoon, to keep his troops sharp and provide work for his 16-man pitching staff, which had to be trimmed to 11 in a few weeks.

Middlesworth would start his report of the intrasquad game this way:

CONTINUED ON PAGE 84

SCOTT ROVAK

As the AL's honorary captain in 2007, Al Kaline stopped for an interview with Marjorie Johnson, cooking correspondent for "The Tonight Show with Jay Leno." Willie Mays served for the National League. The AL won, 5-4, at San Francisco's AT&T Park. Tigers Maggio Ordonez, Placido Polanco and Pudge Rodriguez started and Justin Verlander relieved.

CONTINUED FROM PAGE 83
"Al Kaline just can't quit hitting home runs."

The first time up, against right-hander Duke Maas, Kaline belted a 1-1 curveball, again, into the lower leftfield stands. Ferris Fain, awaiting his turn at the plate, threw his bat high in the air in mock disgust. "I give up," he shouted as Kaline circled the bases.

After Tuesday's off day, the Tigers were rained out Wednesday. Against the White Sox on Thursday, despite a three-day official layoff, Kaline hit yet another home run — and this one counted. But the Tigers were losing, 9-0, when he hit what the Free Press called "a hefty home run into the upper leftfield seats in the sixth." The paper decreed, though, Kaline's homer "was lost in the shuffle." The Tigers managed only four other hits off Mike Fornieles. And George Kell, a former Tiger and Kaline's future partner in the broadcast booth, smacked a grand slam for Chicago, for a 5-0 lead in the top of the third inning.

In Kaline's 22-year career, he hit two homers in a game another 22 times — the final time at age 36 on May 19, 1971, at Cleveland — but he never reached three again. His 399 homers were the result of one three-homer game, 22 two-homer games and 352 one-homer games.

On one leg, Kaline delivers for the AL

It's the 'Other League' 5, Kaline 3

— Detroit Free Press headline

Eighteen times Al Kaline was asked to don his Tigers threads for baseball's All-Star Game — the first time in 1955 as a 20-year-old heading to the batting crown and the last time in 1974 as a 39-year-old zeroing in on his 3,000th hit.

Despite an all-star resume as an American League all-star, Kaline's best performance in a midsummer classic came when he barely could run, on a sweltering nearly 100-degree afternoon in Kansas City on July 11, 1960. He accounted for all three runs in the AL's 5-3 loss — and was on deck with two runners on when former teammate Harvey Kuenn made the final out.

"Al Kaline on one leg is still a good man to have around in the clutch," Hal Middlesworth wrote in the Free Press. "Kaline disclosed just before the game that he hurt his left leg, at the back just above the knee, while running out a double the previous day in the Tigers' 12-10 victory over the Athletics in Kansas City. But he refused to tell Al Lopez, manager of the American League forces, about it."

Why not? Kaline told the press: "Mickey Mantle's having trouble with his knee. Al may need me, and I'll try to make it if I can."

Kaline had been bothered by a sore left knee of his own nearly all season

— and a swing that had deserted him. In late June, his average fell to .225. At the All-Star break, he was hitting only .248 with nine homers and 38 RBIs. He wasn't elected by the players and coaches to the AL all-stars, who would play in Kansas City and then two days later at Yankee Stadium. But Lopez, skipper of the Chicago White Sox, picked him as a reserve. "How can you play an All-Star Game," Lopez said, "without Kaline in it?" Although Kaline was only 25 years old, he had played in six All-Star Games.

The National League built a 5-0 lead by the third inning. The AL had managed a lone single through five innings when Lopez replaced seven of his eight starting position players. Kaline went to centerfield for Mantle, whose two walks accounted for two of the AL's five baserunners.

With one out in the bottom of the sixth inning and Mike McCormick pitching, NL third baseman Eddie Mathews knocked down a wallop by Kaline but his throw couldn't beat the gimpy Tiger. Kaline gritted his way to third on Bill Skowron's single to right. After Elston Howard drew a walk to load the bases, Kaline made it home on Nellie Fox's bloop single

for the AL's first run.

In the top of the next inning, Middlesworth wrote, Kaline "made a thrilling run toward rightfield to haul down Hank Aaron's bid for an extra-base hit."

In the bottom of the eighth, the NL turned to Bob Buhl of the Milwaukee Braves, a right-hander from Saginaw, Michigan. Kuenn, traded by the Tigers to Cleveland for Rocky Colavito three months earlier, reached on an infield throwing error. Kaline followed with a line-drive homer to leftfield, cutting the AL deficit to 5-3. Middlesworth wrote that Kaline "happily limped across the plate behind his former teammate." Kaline had homered the previous year against another Brave, Lew Burdette.

Buhl retired the next three batters and the leadoff batter in the bottom of the ninth. Then Jim Gentile singled and Jim Lemon walked. But Vern Law replaced Buhl and retired Brooks Robinson on a fly to centerfielder Vada Pinson and, with Kaline in the on-deck circle, Kuenn on a liner to rightfielder Roberto Clemente.

Kaline played in the midsummer classic 16 times — injuries sidelined him in 1964 and 1967. He finished with a .324/.375/.514 slash line — 12-for-37 with one double, two homers, six RBIs, seven runs, two walks, one steal, one hit-by-pitch and six strikeouts. He had an .889 OPS (on-base plus slugging).

Only six players have been selected for more All-Star Games: Henry Aaron (25), Willie Mays (24), Stan Musial (24), Mantle (20), Cal Ripken Jr. (19) and Ted Williams (19). Only 11 players have come to bat more often than his 40 plate appearances. Only 10 players have more than his 12 hits and his six RBIs. Only four players have more than his seven runs scored.

– Gene Myers

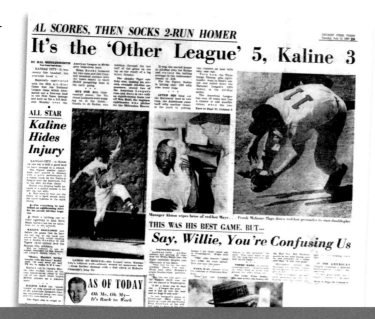

In his toughest season, Mr. Tiger comes through in the clutch to score the pennant-winning run

In a pinch

Exuberant youths aboard a commandeered truck motored through downtown Detroit after the Tigers clinched the 1968 pennant. The Free Press wrote: "Baseball madness. A bedlam of celebration. A riot of happiness. Call it what you like. ... Fans danced and roared through the streets, stood on trash cans and howled in delight, and just generally reveled until the wee hours. The baseball drought was over."

IRA ROSENBERG

BY GENE MYERS

At first glance, the ending was simply storybook. In his 16th season as a perennial all-star for a franchise that finished an average of 18.4 games out of first place from 1953-67, Al Kaline joyfully skipped and hopped as he crossed home plate with the run, in the bottom of the ninth, that clinched the 1968 pennant for the Tigers.

The weight of all the losses, all the injuries, all the criticism, all the expectations, all the self-doubts must have vanished for Kaline, at least for 90 feet. His run on Sept. 17, 1968, set off wild celebrations on the field, in the stands and, soon, in the clubhouse at Tiger Stadium and wilder ones throughout the Motor City. But who possibly could know everything Kaline felt?

A few months from his 34th birthday, Kaline finally realized his dream of playing in a World Series. In the clubhouse, he fought to hold back tears — and he fought to open the celebratory champagne. "I've waited 16 years for this moment," he said,

"and now I can't get the damned cork out!"

In a live TV interview, amid players and team officials covered in champagne and shaving cream, George Kell gushed to his future broadcast partner: "You just had to be the man to score the winning run that capped it all. It had to be that way."

"I had a feeling all day long that I was going to be the one to help win it," Kaline said. "I didn't know whether I'd get in the game or not. And I mentioned that on the bench that if I got in there, I'd help win it some way. ... It's a big thrill. We've been waiting a long time, everybody in Detroit, I have. It's a tremendous feeling."

For Kaline, the Tigers' first pennant since 1945 came that September 1968 day with an incredible backstory of happiness, sadness and duty. And with a dose of fake news.

The Tigers took the lead for good in the American League on May 10. They needed a month to stretch it to five games. They mostly kept it at six, seven or eight games throughout the

CONTINUED ON PAGE 89

The Tigers' road to St. Louis

Before the Tigers could beat the defending champion St. Louis Cardinals in the 1968 World Series, they had to win the American League. The 1968 season was notable because it was the last before the leagues spilt into divisions and expanded the playoffs and because it was the most pitching-dominant year in the modern era.

The season opened April 10 at Tiger Stadium against the Boston Red Sox, the defending AL champs. The Tigers lost, 7-3, but won their next nine games. On April 18, for the first time, the Tigers had a share of first place. On May 3, they fell a half-game behind the Baltimore Orioles but regained the lead on May 10. They never trailed again. A look at the AL standings at key points:

DETROIT FREE PRESS

Sock It To 'Em! Tigers fans celebrate the first pennant since 1945.

MAY 1

TEAM	W-L	PCT	GB
Detroit	13-5	.722	—
Baltimore	11-6	.647	1.5
Minnesota	11-7	.611	2.0
Washington	11-8	.579	2.5
California	9-10	.474	4.5
Boston	8-9	.471	4.5
N.Y. Yankees	8-10	.444	5.0
Oakland	8-11	.421	5.5
Cleveland	7-11	.389	6.0
Chicago W.S.	3-12	.200	8.5

JUNE 1

TEAM	W-L	PCT	GB
Detroit	29-16	.644	—
Baltimore	26-20	.565	3.5
Cleveland	26-21	.553	4.0
Minnesota	24-22	.522	5.5
Boston	23-23	.500	6.5
Oakland	22-24	.478	7.5
California	22-26	.458	8.5
N.Y. Yankees	21-25	.457	8.5
Chicago W.S.	19-25	.432	9.5
Washington	18-28	.391	11.5

JULY 1

TEAM	W-L	PCT	GB
Detroit	49-27	.645	—
Cleveland	43-36	.544	7.5
Baltimore	38-35	.521	9.5
Minnesota	38-36	.514	10.0
Oakland	38-37	.507	10.5
California	37-39	.487	12.0
Boston	36-38	.486	12.0
N.Y. Yankees	33-40	.452	14.5
Chicago W.S.	32-40	.444	15.0
Washington	28-44	.389	19.0

AUG. 1

TEAM	W-L	PCT	GB
Detroit	65-40	.619	—
Baltimore	58-45	.563	6.0
Cleveland	58-49	.542	8.0
Boston	54-49	.524	10.0
Oakland	53-51	.510	11.5
N.Y. Yankees	49-52	.485	14.0
Minnesota	49-54	.476	15.0
California	48-56	.462	16.5
Chicago W.S.	45-56	.446	18.0
Washington	37-64	.366	26.0

SEPT. 1

TEAM	W-L	PCT	GB
Detroit	86-51	.628	—
Baltimore	79-58	.577	7.0
Boston	74-64	.536	12.5
Cleveland	73-68	.518	15.0
Oakland	70-68	.507	16.5
N.Y. Yankees	68-68	.500	17.5
Minnesota	66-72	.478	20.5
California	61-78	.439	26.0
Chicago W.S.	58-79	.423	28.0
Washington	53-82	.393	32.0

FINAL STANDINGS

TEAM	W-L	PCT	GB
Detroit	103-59	.636	—
Baltimore	91-71	.577	12.0
Cleveland	86-75	.534	16.5
Boston	86-76	.531	17.0
N.Y. Yankees	83-79	.512	20.0
Oakland	82-80	.506	21.0
Minnesota	79-83	.488	24.0
California	67-95	.414	36.0
Chicago W.S.	67-95	.414	36.0
Washington	65-96	.404	37.5

DETROIT FREE PRESS

After Joe Sparma delivered a complete game on clinching night, Norm Cash declared: "He's the guttiest guy in this clubhouse. He has intestinal fortitude — you can tell I went to college four years." (Cash had — as a halfback.)

CONTINUED FROM PAGE 87

summer, until the Baltimore Orioles closed within four games on Aug. 27. But when the Tigers took two of three from the O's at Tiger Stadium, their lead was back to seven on Sept. 1.

At that point, the Tigers' eighth pennant seemed inevitable and the rest of the month turned into a countdown to the World Series.

The Tigers' first chance to clinch came on Sept. 16. They were 10½ games ahead of the Orioles (and 17 ahead of the third-place Yankees and Indians). The Tigers crushed the Yankees at Michigan and Trumbull, 9-1, led by Norm Cash's 22nd homer and five RBIs and John Hiller's eight-hitter. That clinched at least a share of the pennant. But the Orioles stayed alive with an 8-1 victory in Boston.

On Sept. 17, a Tuesday, a Tigers victory or an Orioles loss would lead to a citywide celebration. The Orioles-Red Sox game was scheduled

to start a half-hour before the Tigers-Yankees, which meant there was a decent chance Detroit would be the champion before the final out at Tiger Stadium.

Detroit's starting nod fell to right-hander Earl Wilson, a 13-game winner with a 2.85 earned-run average coming off a shutout. Baltimore's hopes to live another day rested with Dave McNally, a 20-game winner who six years later would surrender Kaline's 3,000th hit.

Before that night's game, Kaline went to see manager Mayo Smith and closed his office door. Halfway through the season's final month, Kaline had played in only five September games and come to the plate only 15 times. He wanted to have a heart-to-heart talk with his skipper.

The day after the pennant-clincher, Joe Falls wrote in the Free Press:

"Kaline has been a forlorn figure on the bench. He pitches batting

practice, works out at third base and first base and hits with the scrubs — a strange sight for a player earning $75,000 a year.

"But he has never uttered a word of complaint."

In his age-33 season, Kaline opened in his usual stomping ground in rightfield. He started 37 of the first 39 games as the Tigers built a small lead in the standings. His statistics weren't all-star caliber, but in the Year of the Pitcher his .751 OPS (on-base plus slugging) was at least average. He was hitting .257 with three homers and 16 RBIs when he suffered a broken forearm from a Lew Krausse pitch May 25 in Oakland.

When Kaline returned July 1, after 37 games, the Tigers had built a 7½-game lead on the Indians and 8½ on the Orioles. Jim Northrup started 36 of the 37 games in right, and although he hit only .213 during that stretch, his five homers and 31 RBIs convinced Smith he should be the rightfielder.

Kaline, suddenly, was a first baseman, platooning with the lefty Cash. From time to time, Kaline picked up a game in rightfield when Smith needed a fourth outfielder. At other times, Kaline entered as a pinch hitter and maybe stayed for the finish.

Although an elder statesman without a full-time position, Kaline appeared in nearly every game and posted stellar statistics. From July 1 to Aug. 25, in 46 games and 35 starts, he hit .295 with five homers and 29 RBIs. His OPS was an outstanding .840.

But Kaline tweaked a leg muscle running out a double in the opener of an Aug. 25 doubleheader in New York. He aggravated it pinch-hitting in the ninth inning of the nightcap, forced to exit with a 2-1 count. He played once over the next nine days.

And he hardly played at all when healthy as the Tigers' magic number dwindled to single digits.

Before the clincher, Kaline talked

CONTINUED ON PAGE 90

CONTINUED FROM PAGE 89

in his Franklin, Michigan, home with Falls, the Free Press' sports editor. "I don't deserve to play in the World Series," Kaline told him.

Falls printed his words two days after the clincher. He wrote: "The words tore at Al Kaline's heart as he spoke. You could see the hurt in his eyes."

Kaline added: "It's killing me, but I know what Mayo Smith is up against. I've waited all my life to get into the World Series, but he's got to go with the kids. They deserve the chance to play — they're the ones who have been winning the pennant. I don't see how Mayo can put them on the bench."

Kaline went to the manager's office on Sept. 17 to tell Smith the same thing.

"That shows you what kind of man Al Kaline is," Smith said the day after the clincher. "It's one thing for him to tell that to a reporter, but it's something else for him to come in and tell me. Keeping him on the bench has been the toughest thing I have ever had to do in my life. ...

"When I first came to the Tigers, I heard a lot of derogatory things about Al Kaline — that he wasn't a team player, that he was an individualist, that he thought only of himself ... that he was hard to get along with.

"Well, just the opposite has been true and this shows you what kind of a professional he is."

On Sept. 17, hoping to clinch the pennant, Smith left Kaline on the bench and penciled in his usual lineup against the Yankees: Dick McAuliffe at second, Mickey Stanley in center, Northrup in right, Willie Horton in left, Cash at first, Bill Freehan at catcher, Tommy Matchick at short (he had beaten out the even lighter-hitting Ray Oyler in September) and Don Wert at third.

During warm-ups, however, Wilson felt a twinge in his shoulder. Fans booed right-hander Joe Sparma when his name was announced as

the fill-in. Considered the season's biggest disappointment, Sparma hadn't won since late July, hadn't gone farther than 5 1/3 innings in his last six starts and was dumped from the rotation because of an 8-10 record with a 3.90 ERA. He had pitched only 10 1/3 innings in the five weeks

since declaring that Smith "humiliated" him with a fourth-inning removal in Cleveland before surrendering a run.

All Sparma did against the Yankees was carry a three-hit shutout into the ninth inning. Plus, his fifth-inning

CONTINUED ON PAGE 94

DETROIT TIGERS

The 1968 Tigers won a franchise-record 103 games (later broken by the 1984 squad), scored the most runs (4.09 a game) and surrendered the fewest (3.00). The Tigers finished 12 games ahead of second-place Baltimore; Detroit's seven previous pennants were won by an average of 2.6 games. Al Kaline was in the first row, second from the left. To his right was third baseman Don Wert; to his left was third-base coach Tony Cuccinello.

The injuries and agony of a Hall of Fame healer

Al Kaline passed two milestones early in the 1968 season. He played in his 2,000th game. He hit his 307th home run to break Hank Greenberg's club record. Plus, the Tigers were humming along, on a mission after losing the pennant to Boston on the final day of the 1967 season.

Then misfortune found Kaline — an annual event for a decade.

Although Kaline set an American League record by playing at least 100 games for 20 seasons, he also missed more than 500 games because of a litany of injuries. That's more than three seasons on the sidelines.

On May 25, 1968, at Oakland-Alameda County Coliseum, a pitch from Lew Krausse broke Kaline's forearm. By the time Kaline returned in July, the Tigers had amassed a 7½-game lead and Jim Northrup had swiped his job in rightfield.

Kaline's ailments really started as a child. Because of osteomyelitis, two inches of bone were removed from his left foot, causing a deformity and pain throughout his life. He learned to run on the side of his foot.

In 1959, Kaline suffered a broken cheekbone in his hometown of Baltimore racing to first base to beat a double-play throw. Kaline did — because Billy Gardner's wild throw struck him in the face. Trainer Jack Homel raced out with smelling salts and called for the stretcher.

In a scene that would never happen today, a few hours later, the press corps were allowed in Kaline's hospital room for photos and interviews with the doctor and the patient. Kaline couldn't do much more than mumble short answers.

Within a week, Kaline was back in the lineup. When manager Jimmy Dykes expressed concerned about Kaline's still swollen face, his centerfielder replied: "I don't bat or throw with my cheek."

In 1960, Kaline battled a sore left knee and leg all season. He kept playing, but posted the worst numbers of his prime: .278, 15 homers, 68 RBIs.

In 1962, Kaline appeared poised for a career year. On May 26, he was hitting .340 with remarkable power — 13 homers and 38 RBIs. With two outs in the ninth at Yankee Stadium and the tying run on base, Kaline raced after Elston Howard's short fly in rightfield. Kaline caught the ball just before it hit the ground, then tumbled over, turning a complete somersault — and breaking his right collarbone. Hours later at the hospital, he told the Free Press' Joe Falls: "I guess I'm going to have to become a switch eater and begin using my left hand." In 100 games, Kaline still hit 29 homers — his career high — and drove in 94 runs.

In 1963, another knee injury bothered Kaline all season, when he lost the batting title to Boston's Carl Yastrzemski, .321-.312, but hit 27 homers, drove in 101 runs and finished second in the MVP voting to the Yankees' Howard.

In 1964, Kaline hurt his deformed foot in spring training; it hurt so bad he skipped the All-Star Game but still limped through 146 games.

In 1965, a special shoe helped his foot a bit but not enough. In August, he hurt his ribs attempting a catch. "Well, here I am on the floor again," he said on a stretcher in the first-aid room under the Tiger Stadium stands. For the fourth time, an ambulance took him from a ballpark to a hospital. He missed 15 games.

Off-season surgery on his foot ended two seasons of agony in 1966. He

played in 142 games — a figure he wouldn't come close to until his last season — and hit 29 homers again.

In 1967, Kaline missed a month in the first down-to-the-wire pennant race of his career. When he slammed his bat into the rack after striking

CONTINUED ON PAGE 93

an inside-the-park grand slam, Kaline was flat on the ground motionless. Northrup said he "got up right away but didn't know what to do — I could tell Al was hurt and I didn't know where the ball had gone."

Brewers bullpen coach Jackie Moore, a friend and former teammate, raced to Kaline. "I could hear him gasping for air, he was choking and turning blue," Moore told reporters. "I realized he had swallowed his tongue, and I tried to pry his jaw open. But the best I could do was get two fingers between his teeth."

Leftfielder Willie Horton, the strongest Tiger, knew what to do and took charge of the situation. He managed to pry open Kaline's clenched jaw. Kaline took a few breaths and his eyes opened. He had no clue what had happened.

"That was something I learned when I used to box," Horton said as he demonstrated his technique. "You put pressure on the nerves on the back of the jaw like this, and that makes the man relax enough to let you pry his mouth open." Still, Kaline bit Horton so hard during his life-saving efforts that it left a scar.

Once again, Kaline departed the field on a stretcher and was hustled to a hospital. He spent a Saturday night there for observation but was back at the stadium for the next afternoon's game.

"I don't remember us hitting," Kaline said. "I sort of remember Willie leaning over me and getting my mouth open, and Dick McAuliffe said I asked him how did you guys get out here so fast."

Kaline missed only Sunday's game.
— **Gene Myers**

CONTINUED FROM PAGE 92
out against Indians fireballer Sam McDowell, Kaline suffered a broken finger. It also cost him an All-Star Game — and he had been the American League's leading vote-getter among players and coaches. Hitting .332 with 15 homers and 53 RBIs at

the time, he finished at .308/28/78 in 131 games.

On May 31, 1970, Kaline nearly died on the warning track in Milwaukee's Country Stadium. Kaline and Northrup collided chasing a drive that each thought he had caught. As Roberto Pena circled the bases with

CONTINUED FROM PAGE 90
single had provided the game's only run.

In the top of the ninth, pinch-hitter Charley Smith led off with a single against Sparma, the ball skipping past a diving Oyler. After Steve Whitaker struck out, pinch-runner Dick Howser moved to second on Horace Clarke's bouncer to McAuliffe. Yankees manager Ralph Houk was ejected for arguing that Clarke should have been called safe. That brought up catcher Jake Gibbs, a lefty batting second in the Yankees' order despite a .220 average. Those things happened all the time in the Year of the Pitcher. Gibbs delivered a single up the middle to tie the game.

For the bottom of the ninth, the Yankees turned to left-hander Steve Hamilton. He struck out Northrup and retired Horton on a grounder.

Although 2-for-3 in the game, Cash suggested to his manager that Kaline should bat for him for a righty-lefty matchup instead of lefty-lefty.

"I asked Mayo if he wanted Kaline to hit for me," Cash told the Detroit News. "That's the kind of a team this is. Al has a better chance to get a hit off Hamilton than I have. Maybe he would have hit a home run. Remember, Al and I are the senior partners on this club."

Pitching carefully, Hamilton walked Kaline on five pitches. Freehan singled to left — and the crowd went into a frenzy.

Smith called on Jim Price to hit for Oyler and his .136 average. But Frank Crosetti, handling Houk's duties, turned to right-hander Lindy McDaniel. The stadium grew louder still when pinch-hitter extraordinaire Gates Brown stepped to the plate for Price. Four balls later the bases were loaded.

Up came Wert, who knew a secret along with his manager and his teammates, unlike the multitude in the ballpark and the fans listening to radio broadcast by Ernie Harwell and Ray Lane.

Wert, noted more for his glove than his bat, had a chance to be as unlikely a hero as Sparma.

Although an all-star for the first time in 1968 as he turned 30, Wert had endured a miserable season at the plate. It only had turned worse after he was beaned June 24 by Cleveland's Hal Kurtz. Wert left on a stretcher and missed eight games — and the incident haunted him.

He came to bat in the bottom of the ninth with a .198 average. But it was far worse than that: His average was only .174 since the beaning.

"I tried not to let it affect me, but it did," Wert told mlive.com in 2013. "But I said I wasn't going to let it change my fielding, and I'm proud that didn't happen."

On McDaniel's second pitch to Wert, Kaline made a break to the plate. He slipped but hustled back to third base safely.

"I thought maybe I could get McDaniel to balk when he saw me out of the corner of his eye," Kaline told the News. "He's too smart."

With a 2-2 count, McDaniel went with a slider and Wert drove the ball between second baseman Clarke and first baseman Mickey Mantle.

"I was looking for a breaking pitch on the 2-2 count," Wert told the News. "Lindy McDaniel usually does that."

Harwell called the decisive sequence this way:

"This big crowd here ready to break loose. Three men on, two men out. Game tied, 1-1, in the ninth inning. McDaniel checking his sign with Jake Gibbs. The tall right-hander ready to go to work again, and the windup, and the pitch ...

"He swings, a line shot, base hit, rightfield, the Tigers win it! Here comes Kaline to score and it's all over! Don Wert singles, the Tigers mob Don, Kaline has scored ... The fans are streaming on the field ...

"And the Tigers have won their first pennant since nineteen hundred and forty-five. Let's listen to the bedlam here at Tiger Stadium!"

Bedlam, indeed, erupted at the old ballpark. "Only the walls of Tiger Stadium remained intact," wrote Max E. Simon of the Detroit News.

Fans ripped up and carried away large swatches of turf and countless seats. They swiped every pennant from the stadium roof expect one.

Fans stole first base — who says you can't do that! — and the plates for the warm-up pitchers. "We guarded home plate," stadium manager Jess Walls said, "and they didn't get that."

"They were so wild," general manager Jim Campbell said, "I thought some of the players might get hurt."

Forty extra grounds crewmen would have to be hired to repair Tiger Stadium for the next day's game.

Campbell knew the same secret as Wert: The Tigers actually were the American League champions 15 minutes before Wert's game-winning hit and Kaline's game-winning run. All the drama in the bottom of the ninth, all the fans cheering like mad in the stadium and all the fans hanging on Harwell's every

CONTINUED ON PAGE 95

In September 2018, Don Wert acknowledged the fans' cheers at Comerica Park during the 50th reunion of the 1968 world champions. Wert drove in the game-winning run in the bottom of the ninth the night the Tigers clinched the AL pennant.

CONTINUED FROM PAGE 94

word … none of it had any bearing on the pennant race.

The Tigers' pennant had been clinched in Boston — when the Orioles lost, 2-0, to the Red Sox. The Bosox scored twice in the first inning — on a single by Luis Alvarado, a triple by Carl Yastrzemski and a double by Ken Harrelson — and Ray Culp fired a five-hit, 12-strikeout shutout.

Campbell made the decision not to post the Baltimore result on the scoreboard or announce it on the radio broadcast.

"We were leading, 1-0, and had one out in the ninth," Campbell told the News. "The phone rang in our box and it was Tom Yawkey, the Boston owner. He said: 'We just beat the Orioles and your club wins the pennant.'"

Campbell talked with Walls, who relayed that police feared fans would swarm the field if they heard the score from Boston.

"We would have put up the Oriole score if our game had gone into the 10th inning," Campbell said. "We didn't want the fans to storm the field while our game was on. We probably would have lost on a forfeit."

By the bottom of the ninth, the players knew the pennant was secure, as their traveling secretary spread the word. "Charley Creedon had come to the bench to tell us," Wert said. "But we still wanted to win the game."

Cash said: "We knew on the bench that we had the pennant. But if we lost to the Yankees it wouldn't be any fun at all."

And the Tigers had plenty of fun in their clubhouse. Besides champagne and shaving cream, the players

dunked anyone and everyone in the whirlpool. Suits or uniforms be damned. Owner John Fetzer. Campbell. Denny McLain, who had won his 30th game three days earlier.

"I've picked up so many guys," Freehan told the News, "I don't think I could lift another one."

Kaline couldn't end his night without a return trip to his manager's office. Kaline and Smith gave each other bear hugs, according to the News' account.

"I'm real happy for you after 16 years," Smith said.

"No happier than I am," Kaline replied.

The true storybook ending for Kaline came in the World Series. In 15 days, he would be the rightfielder for Game 1 in St. Louis. And eight days later, he would uncork champagne — successfully — after Game 7.

A shortened season broke in Detroit's favor thanks to a late hot streak from Mr. Tiger

One last hurrah

BY JIM HAWKINS

Storybook. Strictly storybook.

The Tigers, at long last, became the kings of the American League East. Their 3-1 conquest of the Boston Red Sox convinced the world of that.

But what a climax to The Great Race!

There was Al Kaline, the gallant rightfielder, continuing his one-man pennant crusade by driving home the winning run and then catching Ben Ogilvie's fly for the final out.

There was Dick McAuliffe, the goat of the game when his first-inning error let in the lone Red Sox run, hitting a line-drive double and then scoring the go-ahead run on Kaline's seventh-inning single.

There was Woodie Fryman, the journeyman lefty pitching the biggest game of his life and holding the Red Sox to four hits to give the Tigers their first title of any type in four years.

And there were 50,653 hysterically happy people in the old green seats on Oct. 3, 1972, roaring at the top of their lungs, screaming at every strike as Chuck Seelbach finished up where Fryman left off. And then ripping the place apart.

"Battlers ... that's the only word for them," Tigers manager Billy Martin said, his voice hoarse from talking over the raucous clubhouse. "These guys really showed me something."

He called it "my biggest victory," despite his four World Series championships with the Yankees in 11 big-league seasons and his second division title in three seasons as a

CONTINUED ON PAGE 98

With a whoop and a holler and then a charge, Tigers fans went crazy and swarmed the field after the pennant-clinching victory over Boston. Souvenir hunters ripped up 450 square yards of sod, stole all the bases and the pitching rubber, swiped lightbulbs from the auxiliary scoreboards, tore safety padding off the outfield fences and ripped down screens.
TONY SPINA

The Great Race

In 1972, possibly unfairly and in large part because of greed, the Tigers won the American League East by a half-game over the Boston Red Sox. On April 1, major league players staged their first strike, led by legendary union organizer Marvin Miller. At issue were the owners' contributions to the pension fund and the players' desire for salary arbitration.

The strike lasted the first 13 days of the season. That wiped out 86 games — which were never made up. Why not? The owners wanted the players to feel pain in their wallets for having the gall to disrupt the season. So the players didn't get paid for those 13 days, and the American and National leagues picked up the schedule starting April 15.

That Saturday afternoon at Tiger Stadium, the Tigers beat Boston, 3-2, behind Mickey Lolich's nine-strikeout complete game. Only 31,510 fans, instead of the usual packed house, attended the delayed Opening Day. On Sunday, the Tigers were rained out. On Monday, they had a scheduled travel day.

Instead of a full 162-game schedule, some teams played only 153. The Tigers played 156 — one more than the Red Sox. Detroit finished 86-70, Boston 85-70. If the Red Sox had played a 156th game and won it, the teams would have been tied and would have needed a division-deciding playoff game.

To end the strike, the owners agreed on a $500,000 increase in pension fund payments and the introduction of salary arbitration — the latter of which it could be argued caused salaries to skyrocket even more than free agency.

Despite — or maybe because of — the strike, the AL East featured a wide-open race from April to October. Even in late September, four of the six teams — the Tigers, Red Sox, Orioles and Yankees — had a solid shot at winning the division. On the morning of Sept. 4, the four contenders were separated by a mere half-game. The media dubbed it The Great Race.

— Gene Myers

CONTINUED FROM PAGE 96

big-league manager.

There were still those Oakland A's to contend with in the AL playoffs, starting over the weekend on the West Coast. But on this Tuesday night, all the Tigers wanted to do was celebrate.

The long climb had ended. The Great Race was over. Wednesday afternoon's finale against the Red Sox would be a meaningless matinee. Eye to eye with the Bosox in a best two-out-of-three showdown to settle everything, the Tigers made it in two straight.

Appropriately, the honor of winning the big one went to Fryman — who had saved the Tigers so many times since transferring from Philadelphia in early August — and Kaline — whose 11-game hitting streak helped the Tigers win eight crucial games down the stretch. Fryman would raise his record to 10-3 with a 2.06 earned-run average in the AL — after going 4-10 with a 4.36 ERA with the Phillies in the NL. Kaline went 2-for-4 with an RBI and a run scored, raising his season average to .313, up nearly 40 points in the final two weeks.

But this October evening started out looking like anything but a celebration for the Bengals.

Tommy Harper began the game with a single and then immediately swiped second. With one away, Carl Yastrzemski walked and Reggie Smith bounced to Eddie Brinkman for what looked like a routine double play. But McAuliffe, covering the bag, dropped the throw from Brinkman and Harper hustled home in the midst of the confusion at second base.

Until Luis Aparicio doubled down the third-base line with two gone in the fifth inning, Harper's was the only hit the Red Sox got off Fryman.

But for a long while it looked as if that might be enough as the Tigers failed to break through against Luis Tiant — a late-season savior in his own right with the Bosox — until the sixth inning.

Norm Cash opened that inning with a base on balls, Willie Horton bunted him along, and then Jim Northrup slashed a single to right, scoring Cash with the tying run.

Then in the seventh, it happened — just like in the storybooks.

McAuliffe, the guy wearing the goat horns, slammed a one-out double. And Kaline — who else but the old pro? — came through with a single to leftfield to send the Tigers ahead, 2-1.

Albert William Kaline, two months shy of his 38th birthday, now had hit safely in his last 11 games (a 12th was for ninth-inning defense) — batting an even .500 with 22 hits in 44 trips.

Kaline's single finished Tiant, but the Tigers weren't through quite yet, in part because Kaline advanced to second base on

DETROIT FREE PRESS

Picked off waivers Aug. 2, Woodie Fryman went 10-3 with a 2.06 ERA for Detroit.

CONTINUED ON PAGE 101

Trench warfare on the Eastern front

A look at the AL East standings at key points in the season:

MAY 1

TEAM	W-L	PCT	GB
Detroit	7-4	.636	—
Baltimore	7-6	.538	1.0
Cleveland	6-6	.500	1.5
Boston	4-7	.364	3.0
N.Y. Yankees	4-8	.333	3.5
Milwaukee	3-7	.300	3.5

JUNE 1

TEAM	W-L	PCT	GB
Detroit	21-16	.568	—
Baltimore	20-16	.556	0.5
Cleveland	18-17	.514	2.0
N.Y. Yankees	17-20	.459	4.0
Boston	15-19	.441	4.5
Milwaukee	12-22	.353	7.5

JULY 1

TEAM	W-L	PCT	GB
Detroit	36-28	.563	—
Baltimore	35-29	.547	1.0
N.Y. Yankees	28-34	.452	7.0
Boston	27-34	.443	7.5
Cleveland	27-36	.429	8.5
Milwaukee	26-37	.413	9.5

AUG. 1

TEAM	W-L	PCT	GB
Detroit	55-40	.579	—
Baltimore	52-42	.553	2.5
N.Y. Yankees	47-45	.511	6.5
Boston	47-46	.505	7.0
Cleveland	42-52	.447	12.5
Milwaukee	37-58	.380	18.0

SEPT. 1

TEAM	W-L	PCT	GB
Baltimore	67-57	.540	—
Detroit	67-58	.536	0.5
N.Y. Yankees	66-59	.528	1.5
Boston	64-58	.525	2.0
Cleveland	58-66	.468	9.0
Milwaukee	49-75	.395	18.0

SEPT. 4

TEAM	W-L	PCT	GB
Detroit	69-60	.535	—
Baltimore	69-60	.535	—
Boston	67-59	.532	0.5
N.Y. Yankees	69-61	.531	0.5
Cleveland	60-68	.469	8.5
Milwaukee	52-77	.403	17.0

SEPT. 15

TEAM	W-L	PCT	GB
Boston	74-62	.544	—
Detroit	74-64	.536	1.0
Baltimore	74-65	.532	1.5
N.Y. Yankees	74-65	.532	1.5
Cleveland	63-77	.450	13.0
Milwaukee	58-83	.411	18.5

OCT. 1

TEAM	W-L	PCT	GB
Boston	84-67	.556	—
Detroit	83-69	.546	1.5
N.Y. Yankees	79-71	.527	4.5
Baltimore	78-73	.517	6.0
Cleveland	69-83	.454	15.5
Milwaukee	62-90	.408	22.5

FINAL STANDINGS

TEAM	W-L	PCT	GB
Detroit	86-70	.551	—
Boston	85-70	.548	0.5
Baltimore	80-74	.519	5.0
N.Y. Yankees	79-76	.510	6.5
Cleveland	72-84	.462	14.0
Milwaukee	65-91	.417	21.0

"We could beat the (expletive deleted) (expletive deleted) out of Cy Young if they threw him up there."

– Duke Sims, Tigers catcher, speaking on a live radio broadcast after clinching the AL East title, on whether the Tigers would defeat the AL West champion Oakland A's. The Tigers lost the ALCS in five games.

The greatest #$@&%*! celebration

It took a mighty big man to establish some order in the cork-popping locker room, but the Tigers had just the man — Frank Howard, at 6-feet-8 and maybe 275 pounds.

Howard, a 36-year-old first baseman purchased Aug. 31, 1972, from Texas to platoon with Norm Cash, stood towering over his teammates, a roar coming from deep in that barrel chest.

"Give me a T ... give me an I ... give me a G ... give me an E ... give me an R ... give me an S!" roared the big man, getting the correct response every time. "TIGERS!" he roared again — and then even Big Frank couldn't hold back the floodgates.

Nine inches shorter and 100 pounds lighter, second baseman Dick McAuliffe jumped into Howard's arms while screaming.

That was it. Corks popped. Third baseman Aurelio Rodriguez's cork hit the ceiling on the first try. The television lights went on. The reporters started scribbling frantically at a half-dozen scenes at once.

Shortstop Eddie Brinkman wrapped his arms around Al Kaline, the man who drove home McAuliffe with the winning run in the American League East-deciding 3-1 victory over Boston on Oct. 3, 1972, at Tiger Stadium.

Leftfielder Willie Horton, stripped to the waist and muscles rippling, popped a top, dumped the contents of the champagne bottle over Kaline's head and then threw a bear hug around No. 6.

Kaline declared the Tigers had no doubts about the outcome — even though they trailed, 1-0, for the first five innings.

"We were just trying to build each other up," he said. "That's the way this club is."

Kaline, soon to turn 38, accepted

Teammates for the 1958 Tigers who finished 77-77, manager Billy Martin and rightfielder Al Kaline basked in the glory of the AL East title in 1972. "He does it all — hitting, fielding, running, throwing," Martin said, "and he does it with the extra brilliancy that marks him a super ballplayer."
TONY SPINA

congratulations from all comers, including Sen. Robert Griffin (R-Traverse City).

McAuliffe broke free from a Horton bear hug. Rodriguez carried a bottle of champagne in each hand. Coach Joe Schultz slid along the periphery of the crowded room with two cans of Budweiser. (Schultz gained fame in Jim Bouton's ground-breaking book "Ball Four" for repeatedly telling the old Seattle Pilots to "pound some Budweiser.")

Players like Brinkman, who never had played on a pennant winner — even a half-a-pennant winner — led the celebration in the clubhouse. It was Brinkman who also provided the most memorable interview on live television: "It's a fantastic feeling, not so much for myself but for the rest of the (expletive deleted) guys."

So fantastic, so euphoric that Brinkman didn't catch himself until he was nearly finished with his second reference. "We had to struggle through the whole (expletive deleted) ... the whole time."

A pool feed from the locker room was broadcast on Channels 2, 4 and 7 in Detroit. Channel 7 sportscaster Dave Diles was holding the mic for the shared coverage when Brink-

man uttered his famous words. Diles turned away, smiling wanly, in search of someone else to talk to. Back in the WXYZ-TV studio, sportscaster Al Ackerman grinned on camera: "Obviously that was a live feed from the Tiger dressing room. I don't know what I would have said if I had been that excited. Probably something far worse."

And then wry anchor Bill Bonds came on: "I am asked at least twice a week: 'Mr. Bonds, are the programs at 11 o'clock live or are they taped?'" Dramatic pause. "They're live."

Over on the radio side, WJR-AM (760) newsman Don Howe asked catcher Duke Sims whether the Tigers could take Oakland. His live reply: "We could beat the (expletive deleted) (expletive deleted) out of Cy Young if they threw him up there."

The next day, Brinkman said he was embarrassed by his on-air comments and was sorry it had happened. Sims apologized, too, but was much more philosophical:

"You get in a situation like that and you're liable to say anything. I'm sorry if people were offended, but it's the nature of man to curse."

– Curt Sylvester, Jack Saylor and James Harper

CONTINUED FROM PAGE 98

Dwight Evans' throw home, proving that a keen baseball sense can overcome old legs.

Against Bill Lee, Duke Sims was safe with a single when Aparicio couldn't handle his ground ball to short, and an insurance run scored on a Cash grounder to Yastrzemski at first base. Yaz gloved the ball and started to throw it home, trying to catch Kaline ... and then he dropped it as Boston began to show the pressure of its do-or-die showdown.

Asked how he hit so well against Tiant, a herky-jerky right-hander, Kaline shrugged and replied: "I don't know. It's the first time I've faced him this year — I've always been benched before."

When Rico Petrocelli chased Kaline to the warning track with his one-out fly ball in the eighth — with Yastrzemski waiting on second — Martin brought Seelbach out of the bullpen to save the Tigers' title.

Aurelio Rodriguez made a diving grab of Carlton Fisk's line drive to end the eighth ... Evans and Cecil Cooper fell, victims of Seelbach strikeouts to start the ninth ... and then Kaline — who else but the old pro? — smothered Ogilvie's fly ball to end the game and bring the house down. Kaline kept the ball.

"I've got it right in my locker," he said, grinning to a mob of reporters. "I'll keep it, unless Woodie wants it. If he wants it, he can have it."

While the Tigers raced full speed off the field, the fans swarmed out of their seats to pull up the bases and rip up huge chunks of turf and generally act as if they just had made the playoffs.

As the 1974 season drew to a close, Mr. Tiger reached baseball's most hallowed milestone at last

Mr. 3,000

BY GENE MYERS

Al Kaline can retire in peace.

His all-out season-long quest for that elusive 3,000th hit is over.

It ended Tuesday evening, at 20 minutes past 8 o'clock, in the fourth inning of the 2,827th game of his brilliant 22-year career.

Kaline sliced Dave McNally's first pitch of the fourth inning down the rightfield line for a stand-up double, avoiding the white chalk foul line by less than two feet.

Al also singled during the course of the Tigers' narrow 5-4 defeat at the hands of the pennant-conscious Baltimore Orioles, lifting him past the late Roberto Clemente and into 11th place on baseball's all-time hit parade with 3,001 to his credit.

Those were the words Jim Hawkins of the Free Press used to describe Al Kaline's historic night in Baltimore, his hometown. On Sept. 24, 1974, in Kaline's 140th game of the season — the Tigers' 154th — he delivered his 139th hit of the season (and 140th for good measure) to reach the 3,000-hit club. At the time, Kaline was a little less than three months shy of his 40th birthday.

CONTINUED ON PAGE 104

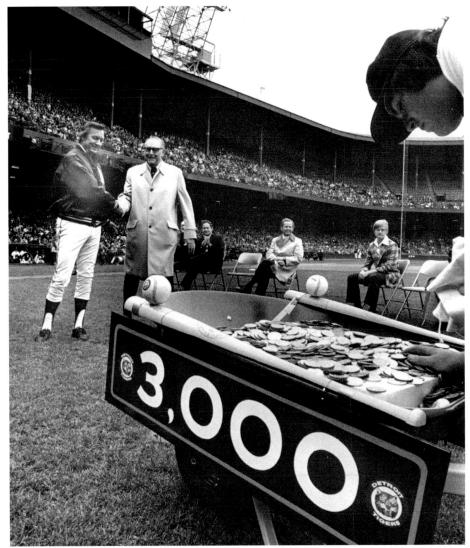

JIMMY TAFOYA

Five days after his 3,000th hit in 1974, the Tigers staged their second Al Kaline Day, four years after the first. On a miserable September afternoon, Kaline had to figure out what to do with 3,000 silver dollars, courtesy of owner John Fetzer.

Ernie Harwell wrote that his favorite Al Kaline story occurred in 1974. Baltimore pitcher Dave McNally wanted a Ford dealership in Montana and asked Kaline in the spring whether he knew anybody who could help. "I knew Lee Iacocca, the president," Kaline told him. "I'll talk to him about you." By midseason, McNally had his dealership. He called to thank Kaline — and told him he dreamed he gave up Kaline's 3,000 hit. On Sept. 24, that dream came true.

MALCOLM EMMONS

It's the President, Al

The day after reaching 3,000 hits, Al Kaline was leaning against the batting cage in Baltimore's Memorial Stadium, patiently waiting for his next turn, when the call came.

It was from President Gerald Ford, a Grand Rapids native and former University of Michigan football player.

"He called to congratulate me and to say he had been pulling for me," Kaline said upon returning to the field from the clubhouse. "He said he knew when I got those three hits in Boston (on Sept. 18) there was no question I'd make it this year."

Kaline met Ford when the Tigers star was campaigning in the state on behalf of former President Richard Nixon. Kaline was a guest of Ford, below right, and Sen. Robert Griffin (R-Traverse City) at Nixon's inauguration. (Griffin, as deputy minority leader in the Senate, helped prod Nixon to resign in August 1974 because of the Watergate scandal.)

"The president said he was very happy for me and that I've been a credit to the game and to the young people of this country," Kaline said. "He invited me to come and see him whenever I'm in Washington."

– Gene Myers

A diamond dozen

How they stood after Al Kaline became the 12th member of the 3,000-hit club on Sept. 24, 1974:

PLAYER	YEARS	3,000	ORDER	HITS
Ty Cobb	1905-28	Aug. 19, 1921	4th	4,189
Stan Musial	1941-63	May 13, 1958	8th	3,630
Hank Aaron	1954-	May 17, 1970	9th	3,596
Tris Speaker	1907-28	May 17, 1925	5th	3,514
Honus Wagner	1897-1917	June 9, 1914	2nd	3,430
Eddie Collins	1906-30	June 3, 1925	6th	3,315
Willie Mays	1951-73	July 18, 1970	10th	3,283
Nap Lajoie	1896-1916	Sept. 27, 1914	3rd	3,243
Paul Waner	1926-45	June 19, 1942	7th	3,152
Cap Anson*	1876-97	July 18, 1897	1st	3,012
Al Kaline	1953-	Sept. 24, 1974	12th	3,001
Roberto Clemente	1955-72	Sept. 30, 1972	11th	3,000

NOTE: Four seasons passed after Kaline's 3,000th hit before another player reached the milestone. Cincinnati's Pete Rose did so on May 5, 1978. St. Louis' Lou Brock was next on Aug. 13, 1979. Boston's Carl Yastrzemski on Sept. 12, 1979, finally, followed Kaline as an American League player to reach the milestone since 1925.

*Also credited with 3,435 hits by baseball-reference.com by including 1871-75 statistics in the National Association, the first pro league.

CONTINUED FROM PAGE 102

As he sat in the clubhouse sipping half a glass of champagne afterward, Kaline admitted that his latest milestone meant even more to him than the batting title he won in 1955 at the unprecedented age of 20.

"This definitely ranks above the batting title," he said, beaming. "Anytime you win a batting championship, there's a lot of luck that goes with it. But when you get 3,000 hits, I don't think anybody can say you were just lucky. You've had to withstand the pressure of all those seasons and injuries and everything. To me that really means something."

Then Kaline added: "But nothing will surpass winning the World Series."

In the first inning, Kaline made the final out with a grounder to shortstop Mark Belanger. The Orioles were in a neck-and-neck final-week race with the Yankees for first place in the East Division; the Tigers, in Baltimore for a two-game series, were dead last in the division.

The Tigers took a 1-0 lead in the third inning. In the fourth, Kaline led off against McNally, who was coming off a shutout for his 16th victory. McNally started Kaline with a fastball and when he hit it, Kaline thought for sure that the ball was going to slice foul.

"I almost forgot to run," Kaline said with a sheepish grin. "The ball was really curving foul. It was plenty fair when I hit it, but I didn't think it was going to make it. When I got to second base I said a little prayer of

CONTINUED ON PAGE 105

In essence, Al Kaline, with Louise, waved goodbye as a player on the second Al Kaline Day in 1974. But Kaline never stopped appearing on the field at Tiger Stadium or Comerica Park in his role as Mr. Tiger, to be honored or to honor others.
JIMMY TAFOYA

Mr. Tiger's hit parade

How Al Kaline reached 3,007 hits in his 22-year career with the Tigers:

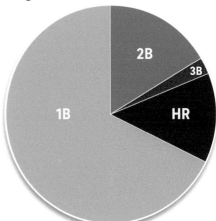

TYPE	NO.
Singles	2,035
Doubles	498
Triples	75
Homers	399
Total	3,007

CONTINUED FROM PAGE 104
thanks for letting me play all these years and get all those hits.

"Once I got this close I knew I'd get the hit sometime, but I'm very glad to get it here. I knew I had a lot of friends and relatives in the stands and I would have hated to disappoint them.

"I'm proud to have been able to get my 3,000th hit off McNally, too. I know he says I've gotten a lot of hits off him, but he must remember more of them than I do. He's a real tough pitcher.

"I don't really remember much of anything at the time of the pitch. I knew it was a fastball. ... It was up a little bit and tailing off some. ...

"I'm just happy it's finally over. It seemed like a big black cloud had been lifted from me as soon I got it."

The festivities following Kaline's historic hit were remarkably brief, primarily because he wanted it that way.

The game was stopped while Kaline, amidst a standing ovation from the crowd of 11,492, walked over to the club box to the right of the Tigers' dugout where members of his family and assembled dignitaries were waiting. After first being embraced

CONTINUED ON PAGE 106

As Al Kaline grew long in the tooth, his crew cut also grew into a more modern hairstyle. It was so bitterly cold in Tiger Stadium he donned gloves during his final game on Oct. 2, 1974. He was two months from his 40th birthday.
ALAN R. KAMUDA

CONTINUED FROM PAGE 105

by his parents, Naomi and Nicholas, Kaline handed his bat and the ball to AL president Lee MacPhail, who would see to it that they made it to Cooperstown.

By 8:23 p.m. — a mere three minutes after the bat met the ball — the whole thing was over, Kaline was back standing on second base and Bill Freehan was waiting for McNally's second pitch of the fourth inning.

Kaline's mission all season had been to reach 3,000 hits before retiring. No player in the American League had accomplished the feat since Eddie Collins on June 5, 1925, nearly a half-century prior.

To assist Kaline's quest, he was employed exclusively as a designated hitter after splitting time between rightfield and first base in recent seasons. To reach the necessary 139 hits, he needed to stay healthy, a rarity for more than a decade, he needed to play nearly every game and he needed more hits than he had accumulated in a season since the mid-1960s.

He would finish the season with 147 games played, 630 plate appearances and 558 at-bats, all his highest totals since 1961. His 146 hits marked his highest total since 1964.

Kaline's 3,001st hit came on his next at-bat, with Ron LeFlore on third base and Gary Sutherland on first base with nobody out in the sixth inning. Kaline's single to center tied that game at 2.

The Orioles regained the lead with a run in the bottom of the inning, but the Tigers went back ahead, 4-3, on a two-run homer by Eddie Brinkman in

CONTINUED ON PAGE 107

CONTINUED FROM PAGE 106

the seventh inning. With Sutherland later on first, McNally was removed for Bob Reynolds, who retired Kaline to end the inning on a fly to left. He would not bat again.

The Orioles won it with a pair of runs in the eighth. Tigers reliever John Hiller was five outs from his 18th victory as a reliever, which would have been a major-league record, when Don Baylor doubled and Brooks Robinson doubled him home, took third on a wild pitch and crossed the plate on Andy Etchebarren's suicide squeeze.

Kaline said he had one more goal: his 400th home run.

"I only need one more for 400 and that's what I'll be going for," he said. "I think, the rest of the year, you'll see me much more aggressive at the plate, now that I've got that 3,000th hit behind me. It feels like a big weight has been lifted off my shoulders, believe me."

The Tigers immediately announced that Kaline would be honored in five days, on a Sunday afternoon at Tiger Stadium, and fans would receive a commemorative poster.

Kaline declined to address his future. The Free Press' Hawkins wrote what eventually came to pass: "Kaline will retire at the end of the season and his plans for the future still aren't solidified. He can just about take his pick of positions with the Tigers, but doesn't know precisely what he wants to do and probably will partially detach himself from baseball for the first year."

Milestone moments

The road to 3,007 for Al Kaline:

⊠ **FIRST HIT:** July 8, 1953, at Chicago — Single through shortstop in the eighth inning off White Sox right-hander Luis Aloma. It was the third at-bat of Kaline's career. The Tigers lost, 14-4. Oddly, each team had 15 hits. Kaline also made the game's final out, on a fly to center.

⊠ **500TH HIT:** Aug. 25, 1956, at Baltimore — A third-inning single to leftfield off Orioles left-hander Don Ferrarese. Kaline went 2-for-4 with an RBI, a run and a walk in a 7-3 Detroit victory.

⊠ **1,000TH HIT:** Aug. 11, 1959, at Detroit — A seventh-inning single off White Sox right-hander Ken McBride. In an 8-1 Tigers victory, Kaline went 2-for-2 with a three-run homer, two walks and a stolen base.

⊠ **1,500TH HIT:** Sept. 20, 1962, at Bloomington, Minn. — A two-run homer off Minnesota Twins left-hander Jim Kaat in the fifth inning. In a 5-1 Tigers victory, Kaline went 3-for-4 with two RBIs, two runs, a walk and a steal.

⊠ **2,000TH HIT:** June 15, 1966, at Boston — A first-inning single to left off Red Sox right-hander Jim Lonborg. It scored a run; Kaline advanced to second on the throw from left. He doubled and scored in the eighth and hit a two-run homer in the ninth. In an 11-7 Tigers victory, Kaline went 3-for-4 with three RBIs, three runs and a walk.

⊠ **2,500TH HIT:** June 5, 1970, at Oakland — A fifth-inning single to center off Athletics right-hander Blue Moon Odom. In a 4-2 Tigers loss, Kaline went 1-for-4 with a run and a walk. He also grounded into a 1-4-3 double play to end the game.

⊠ **3,000TH HIT:** Sept. 24, 1974, at Baltimore — A fourth-inning double down the rightfield line off Orioles left-hander Dave McNally. Kaline had grounded out to short in the first inning. He added hit No. 3,001, a run-scoring single to center, in the sixth inning. He flied out to left in the seventh against Bob Reynolds to finish 2-for-4 with an RBI — the next-to-last in his career — in a 5-4 Tigers loss.

⊠ **LAST HIT (NO. 3,007):** Oct. 1, 1974, at Detroit — An eighth-inning single to center off Orioles right-hander Jim Palmer. Three batters later, Kaline scored the tying run, 6-6, on a Dan Meyer double. The Orioles went ahead, 7-6, in the ninth. With two out and Ron LeFlore on third, Kaline took a called third strike. He finished 1-for-5 with a run. In the season finale the next day, against Orioles left-hander Mike Cuellar, Kaline struck out looking in the first and flied out to left in the third. He asked manager Ralph Houk to remove him when his turn came up in the fifth.

"Anytime you win a batting championship, there's a lot of luck that goes with it. But when you get 3,000 hits, I don't think anybody can say you were just lucky."

Kaline's final bows as an all-star

For the 17th and 18th time in his storied career, Al Kaline was selected for the All-Star Game in the 1970s. The details:

July 13, 1971 — Tiger Stadium, Detroit

AL 6, NL 4: The All-Star Game came to the Motor City for the first time since 1951. This time, it would be played under the lights. At age 36, Kaline was selected more for his longevity and the geography than his statistics (although hitting .303, he had only eight homers and 28 RBIs in 65 starts).

Kaline replaced Frank Robinson in rightfield in the top of the sixth inning, batting cleanup. He went 1-for-2 with a single, a run and a strikeout.

Sixth inning vs. Fergie Jenkins: Leading off with the AL ahead, 4-3, Kaline singled to center. It would be his 12th and final hit in an All-Star Game. He scored when the next batter, Harmon Killebrew, hit a home run to left for a 6-3 lead. After the next batter, Brooks Robinson, singled, the AL's final eight batters produced a walk, two double plays and nine outs. Kaline's run proved to be the game-winner.

Eighth inning vs. Don Wilson: After Carl Yastrzemski's leadoff walk, Kaline struck out. Killebrew hit into a 5-4-3 double play.

"I was hoping to get in for at least an inning or two," Kaline said. "I was glad I did. I really wanted it badly with my boys (Mark and Mike) watching."

The old ballpark that opened in 1912, a few days before the Titanic sank in the North Atlantic, was all decked out in splendor for its third (and final) All-Star Game in July 1971. Al Kaline was selected for the 17th time. Norm Cash started at first base and Bill Freehan as the catcher. Mickey Lolich recorded the save in a 6-4 AL victory. And Kaline singled and scored the decisive run. Fans will never forget Reggie Jackson's missile that struck the light tower atop the rightfield roof.

July 23, 1974 — Three Rivers Stadium, Pittsburgh

NL 7, AL 2: At 39, Kaline announced he would play one more season in an attempt to reach 3,000 hits. To save wear and tear on his body, he would be used exclusively as a designated hitter or pinch hitter. Leading up to the All-Star Game, Kaline said he hoped fans would not vote him as a starting outfielder, since he hadn't been playing there. When they did not — he finished sixth behind Reggie Jackson, Jeff Burroughs, Bobby Murcer, Joe Rudi and Frank Robinson — manager Dick Williams picked Kaline as one of his 12 reserves. He was hitting .251 with four homers and 30 RBIs. Williams also bestowed a longevity honor on Robinson, 38, another DH, hitting .253 with 13 homers and 42 RBIs for the Angels.

Kaline hit for pitcher Gaylord Perry in the fourth inning.

Fourth inning vs. Ken Brett: With the AL ahead, 2-1, with two out and Burroughs on with leadoff walk, Kaline hit a foul pop that catcher Johnny Bench grabbed.

Luis Tiant took the mound for the AL in the bottom of the fourth. Nineteen years after his first appearance, Kaline's all-star resume was complete: 16 games, a .324/.375/.514 slash line, 12-for-37 with one double, two homers, six RBIs, seven runs, two walks, one steal and one hit-by-pitch.

Mr. Tiger didn't have to wait long in retirement — just the five-year minimum — for the highest honor

Called to the Hall

BY JIM HAWKINS AND MICK MCCABE

For 22 years, Al Kaline excelled at the game of baseball in the aged stadium at Michigan and Trumbull. Much of that time he was the Tigers' one and only superstar. Rarely did he receive a superstar's national recognition.

All that changed on Jan. 9, 1980. Kaline was voted a place among baseball's immortals in the Hall of Fame on the very first ballot — making him only the 10th player in history so honored. No longtime Tiger had been elected since Sam Crawford in 1957 — by the veterans committee — and Hank Greenberg in 1956 — by the baseball writers.

"I don't think my vocabulary can express what I feel," Kaline declared at a news conference inside Tiger Stadium. "Knowing all the great players who didn't make it on the first ballot, I thought my chances of making it were nip and tuck, maybe 50-50. So, I tried to stay low key.

"Certainly, the ultimate possible

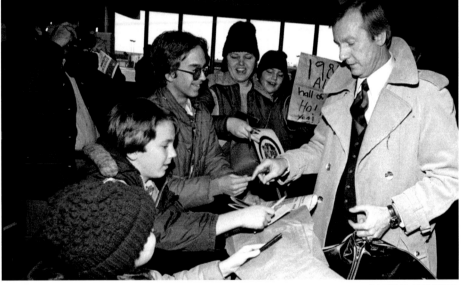

ALAN R. KAMUDA

Fans surrounded Al Kaline at Metro Airport hours after his election to the Hall of Fame was announced in New York. He obliged with autographs, of course.

is to go into the Hall of Fame on the first ballot. It's super just to get in. I really never thought I would choose an individual thing that happened just to me over a team thing like the World Series. But I would have to say this is the biggest thing that has ever happened to me."

Kaline, 45, received votes on 340

of the 385 ballots cast by veteran members of the Baseball Writers' Association of America. In order to be elected, a player needed 289 votes — or 75% of the ballots cast. Kaline received 88.3%.

Also elected was Duke Snider, a Brooklyn and Los Angeles Dodgers

CONTINUED ON PAGE 117

Al Kaline relished his summer trips to Cooperstown for the annual induction ceremonies and to see his old pals.
ERIC SEALS

Kaline takes his place with the immortals of baseball

The skies were gray and rainy for much of Al Kaline's day in the sun.

Then, as he prepared officially and ceremoniously to enter the Baseball Hall of Fame in Cooperstown, New York, the clouds parted as if by script. As Kaline stood on Aug. 3, 1980, with his bronze plaque on the back porch of the National Baseball Library, the sun shone brightly in the blue sky.

Kaline told everyone how happy he was to take his place among the immortals of the national pastime. He spoke with his own solemn joy and only once in 9½ minutes did his voice crack and tears come to his eyes, when he told the 5,000 fans he wanted to thank his parents for their "love and hard work."

He acknowledged all other members of his family and Tigers management, including scout Ed Katalinas who signed him, before he turned to the hundreds of Detroit sports fans on hand.

"Most of all, I'd like to particularly thank Tiger fans everywhere," he said.

The crowd cheered. "But especially those who supported me my entire career in Detroit. We've had our highs and some lows. But through it all, Detroit fans have stuck with the Tigers to prove they are the best in baseball."

In the crowd were former teammates Reno Bertoia, Bill Freehan and Jim Price. Another, Mickey Lolich, stood almost anonymously, wearing sunglasses.

At 45, Kaline, as usual, looked fit and handsome, wearing a light summer suit, blue shirt and tie, with his hair neat and in place.

"I've been very lucky; sometimes, in fact, I feel I have been one of the luckiest people in the world," Kaline said. "I played on All-Star teams with the greatest players in the game. I was able to finish with over 3,000 hits. I played on the world championship team. Most of all, for 22 years, I was able to make a living playing a game that has been my whole life."

– Joe Lapointe

Cooperstown speech: All in the family

During his 9½-minute Hall of Fame induction speech, Al Kaline spent a quarter of it directly addressing his family: Louise, his high school sweetheart and wife of 35 years; Mark and Mike, his sons; and Nicholas and Naomi, his parents. They each stood, received a round of applause and were caught for posterity by the ESPN cameras. From Kaline's speech:

"You'll see that without these people there would be no way I'd be standing here today. First, my lovely wife, Louise. Unless you're in baseball, it's very difficult to understand and appreciate the role a wife plays for a player. For all the time I was on the road and all the evenings in Detroit when I was playing a game, she was at home playing mom and pop to our two sons. For all the support when I was fighting a slump and all the encouragement when I was fortunate to be in a streak, thanks, Louise.

"For all the fame and glory one derives from playing baseball isn't worth a thing without someone to share it with. It must not be easy growing up and going to school while the old man is fighting a batting slump which might hurt the pennant of the home team. But they were always there with words of encouragement, the pride of my life, my sons, Mark and Mike.

"When I was a youngster, life was a baseball game. There was nothing more exciting than a good old game of ball. I played a lot of ball games growing up in Baltimore, every day from spring to fall. I never would have had that chance to prepare for a career every boy dreams of without the love and hard work of two people, my mom and dad."

The ballot box

To be elected to baseball's Hall of Fame in 1980, players needed to appear on 289 out of 385 ballots (75%) by members of the Baseball Writers' Association of America. Only Al Kaline (88.3%) and Duke Snider (86.5%) met that requirement. Here's who received votes in 1980 (players later elected by the BBWAA or a veterans committee appear in bold type):

PLAYER	YEAR	VOTES	PCT
Al Kaline	1	340	88.3%
Duke Snider	11	333	86.5%
Don Drysdale	6	238	61.8%
Gil Hodges	12	230	59.7%
Hoyt Wilhelm	3	209	54.3%
Jim Bunning	4	177	46%
Red Schoendienst	12	164	42.6%
Nellie Fox	10	161	41.8%
Maury Wills	3	146	37.9%
Richie Ashburn	13	134	34.8%
Luis Aparicio	2	124	32.2%
Roger Maris	7	111	28.8%
Mickey Vernon	15	96	24.9%
Harvey Kuehn	4	83	21.6%
Lew Burdette	8	66	17.1%
Don Newcombe	15	59	15.3%
Ted Kluszewski	14	50	13%
Orlando Cepeda	1	48	12.5%
Alvin Dark	15	43	11.2%
Bill Mazeroski	3	33	8.6%
Don Larsen	7	31	8.1%
Elston Howard	7	29	7.5%
Elroy Face	5	21	5.5%
Ron Santo	1	15	3.9%
Norm Cash	1	6	1.6%
Matty Alou	1	5	1.3%
Felipe Alou	1	3	0.8%
Mel Stottlemyre	1	3	0.8%
Steve Blass	1	2	0.5%
Dick Green	1	1	0.3%
Jim Hickman	1	1	0.3%
Sonny Jackson	1	1	0.3%
Don McMahon	1	1	0.3%

Mementos from Al Kaline's playing days were treated with TLC to preserve them for generations to come.
RICHARD LEE

TIM CLARY

Al Kaline donned his fancy attire for a Baltimore awards dinner with his wife, Louise, and his parents, Naomi and Nicholas.

In 1970 and again in 1974, it's Al Kaline Day at The Corner

The speeches, the standing ovations, the street signs for Al Kaline. They were better than a double dose of Geritol.

"You know, right now, I feel five years younger," Kaline exclaimed with a grin when he finally stepped into the shade of the Tiger Stadium dugout after almost an hour's worth of Al Kaline Day ceremonies in the hot sun on Aug. 2, 1970.

You would have thought, after the speeches packed with superlatives and the slow ride around the stadium, serenaded by Mel Torme's "Thanks for the Memories," plus more standing ovations from the fans in each section he passed, that Kaline would have been worn out. And that was before the game even began.

And Kaline admitted that he was — but it felt great.

They rewrote a song in his honor. They renamed streets in Lakeland, Florida, and around the old ballpark. They loaded him down with mostly symbolic gifts, including a letter from President Richard Nixon, a clock from his fellow Tigers and $20,000 in college scholarships for his two young sons from owner John Fetzer.

All because, for most of his 18 years in a Tigers uniform and now at age 35, Al Kaline had been Mr. Tiger, serving under 11 managers and outlasting three U.S. presidents.

And then, after the mayor and governor and the others had finished saying all those nice things about him, Kaline stepped up to the battery of microphones.

"I know I should have had a speech prepared," he began, "but sometimes, you know, you can't remember the words that you've been

thinking about for almost a month. I do want to thank everyone here on the field and everyone who has participated in these ceremonies and has worked so hard to make this a very great day ... the greatest day in my life. ...

"This day I'll always remember."

And then he got to do it all over again. The Tigers staged their second Al Kaline Day on Sept. 29, 1974, a cold and windy Sunday afternoon five days after his 3,000th hit and three days from end of his final season.

The 21,178 fans paid tribute with no less than five standing ovations, the longest lasting almost two minutes. Still, somehow, it seemed almost anticlimactic. Kaline, now 39, felt it, too.

"When they talked about having this day for me," Kaline said, "I didn't particularly want one. Don't misunderstand. I appreciate all that everyone has done for me. I thought the whole thing was handled very well. It was really nice. And it was very refreshing to see all those people show up on such a bad day.

"Sure, I was a little emotional — but it wasn't like the last day they had for me. That was much more emotional for me and my family.

"I guess when you shoot for something like I did for 3,000 hits, when you push all year, when you finally get it, there's bound to be a letdown. I know, right now, I'm very relaxed. Probably more so than I should be.

"I don't feel any emotion at all about quitting. As a matter of fact, I can't wait."

The Free Press noted two unexpected absences for the festivities: baseball commissioner Bowie Kuhn and Detroit Mayor Coleman Young. Michigan Gov. William Milliken was

on hand, as was Carl Levin, president of the Common Council, and Billy Rogell, the former Tiger turned councilman.

Fetzer gave Kaline 3,000 silver dollars.

"That gift really shocked me," said Kaline, who did not note that with two more hits in that day's game his boss was actually $6 short.

— **Jim Hawkins**

ALAN R. KAMUDA

Pinch-hitter extraordinaire Gates Brown, in uniform as Sparky Anderson's batting coach, congratulated his longtime teammate when the Tigers retired Al Kaline's number in August 1980. They played together from 1963-74.

The initial number: No. 6 retired by Tigers

After Al Kaline flew from a news conference in New York to a news conference in Detroit following his election to the Hall of Fame, Tigers general manager Jim Campbell announced that the ballclub would break with tradition and retire Kaline's No. 6.

No previous Tigers uniform numbers had been retired because Ty Cobb, the legendary centerfielder (and bad boy), never wore a number during his Detroit days (1905-26). Tigers management never felt any player should be honored above Cobb — until Kaline (a good guy) in 1980.

Two weeks after his induction, on Aug. 17, 1980, Kaline was back on the field at Tiger Stadium — with his wife, Louise, other family members and 35 former Tigers. He received his No. 6 jersey and held it aloft to the four corners of the old ballpark, waving and smiling. The 42,117 fans responded with loud screams and stamping feet.

Kaline told the roaring crowd in a short speech that he was "one of the luckiest baseball players that ever lived" for having spent his entire 22-year career in Detroit, "the greatest baseball town in the major leagues."

"It made my career more enjoyable," he said, "than any player has a right to expect."

During the ceremony, Pat Mullin, whose final year in the Tigers' outfield was Kaline's first, told about the "tall, skinny kid with a crew cut" in 1953 who asked for his No. 6 when he retired. "You served the uniform well," Mullin told Kaline.

Kaline, who initially wore No. 25, said he wanted No. 6 or No. 9 because they were the numbers worn by his two heroes, Stan Musial of the Cardinals and Ted Williams of the Red Sox.

"Many players take their uniforms for granted," Kaline said. "I never did. Every time I put on the Tiger uniform, I did it with pride."

— Bill McGraw

MIKE MCCLURE

Wife Louise received a beautiful bouquet and son Mike a loving hug on Al Kaline Day in August 1970. A 4-3 Tigers loss ended with two men on base and Kaline on deck. "Don't forget I've been watching his act for 10 years," Twins manager Bill Rigney said. "I didn't want him coming up and ruining *my* day."

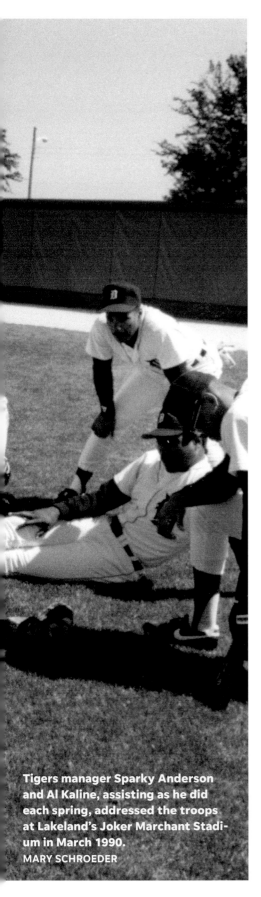

Tigers manager Sparky Anderson and Al Kaline, assisting as he did each spring, addressed the troops at Lakeland's Joker Marchant Stadium in March 1990.
MARY SCHROEDER

CONTINUED FROM PAGE 110

centerfielder. On his 11th year of a possible 15 on the ballot, he received 333 votes (86.5%).

No one else came close. Rounding out the top 10: Dodgers pitcher Don Drysdale (sixth year on the ballot), 61.8%; Dodgers first baseman Gil Hodges (12th year), 59.7%; Dodgers knuckleballer Hoyt Wilhelm (third year), 54.3%; Tigers right-hander Jim Bunning (fourth year), 46%; Cardinals second baseman Red Schoendienst (12th year), 42.6%; White Sox second baseman Nellie Fox (10th year), 41.8%; Dodgers shortstop Maury Wills (third year), 37.9%; and Phillies centerfielder Richie Ashburn (13th year), 34.8%. (Of the also-rans, each player eventually made the Hall of Fame, via a BBWAA election or a veterans committee, except Hodges and Wills.)

Since the Hall of Fame opened in Cooperstown, New York, in 1936, only nine other players had received the votes necessary to be elected the first time their names appeared on the ballot: Jackie Robinson (1962), Bob Feller (1962), Ted Williams (1966), Stan Musial (1969), Sandy Koufax (1972), Warren Spahn (1973), Mickey Mantle (1974), Ernie Banks (1977) and Willie Mays (1979).

In addition, Babe Ruth, Ty Cobb, Walter Johnson, Christy Mathewson and Honus Wagner were ushered in immediately in 1936.

"There were some great players like Joe DiMaggio that didn't make it on the first ballot," Kaline said. "I was prepared for anything. I certainly wouldn't have been embarrassed by any means if I hadn't made it."

Kaline's call of a lifetime — from BBWAA president Jack Lang — came at 6:25 p.m. on Jan. 8, a Tuesday. On Wednesday afternoon, Kaline recounted how everything unfolded to a Free Press reporter during a flight from New York to Detroit and how the BBWAA and Hall of Fame desperately wanted to keep the election results under wraps for nearly 18 hours.

Lang "told us he would call about 6 p.m. to tell us if I made it or not," Kaline recalled. "I was getting all these people calling then and I was trying to get them off the phone. Television stations wanted to do live interviews, but I told them I couldn't.

"We were laughing every time the phone rang. My son Mike was trying to predict what time we'd get THE call. Then Jack called and said: 'Congratulations, you made it.' It was just like that.

"I said, 'I don't believe it!' and then my wife started yelling. It's hard to believe I made it on the first ballot."

Kaline called his parents, Naomi, 73, and Nicholas, 78, in Baltimore. Kaline swore his mother to secrecy; she didn't even tell his two older sisters, who were visiting their parents at the time.

"We at least wanted to live till Al got in the Hall of Fame," Naomi told the Free Press the next day. "We started saving money a year ago to go to Cooperstown. You know, I don't talk much. I haven't talked that much about Al. But I'm glad to talk about him today."

Kaline also called his eldest son, Mark, who worked with a radio station in Jackson, Michigan.

"I told Mark he couldn't tell anyone about this," Kaline said on the plane. "I told him he could have gotten me in a lot of trouble if he would have told his station. Channel 4 wanted an exclusive, but I told them I couldn't give it to them."

Kaline, of course, handled color commentary on Tigers telecasts shown by Channel 4 (WDIV-TV) in Detroit.

Kaline's next order of business was a night flight to New York. He traveled with his wife, Louise, on the passenger list as Mr. and Mrs. Al Hamilton, his wife's maiden name.

"We couldn't even register at the hotel," Kaline said. "We had to go up to Jack's suite. He had a three-bed-

CONTINUED ON PAGE 121

Kaline's second career: A 26-year trial in the booth

After 22 seasons as a Tiger, 3,007 base hits and 1½ years in retirement, Al Kaline decided to return to baseball. On a trial basis.

He agreed to join the Tigers' television broadcast team for six games early in the 1976 season. The announcement came two days before the April 10 opener at Cleveland. Kaline, now 41, would be on the air with George Kell and Larry Osterman.

"I told them I'd like to see how I like it — and how they like me," said Kaline, who had considerable success as a manufacturer's representative in retirement. "Then we can make a decision on the rest of the year.

"I really don't know how well I'm going to do. That's why I want to try it first. I don't think it'll be that hard. But until you try something, you never know."

Kaline's six games turned into 26 seasons — four more than he spent on the field.

Kaline and Kell, each inducted into the Hall of Fame during their many years together in the booth, became beloved fixtures for fans, just as Ernie Harwell and Paul Carey did in the radio booth.

"I know how hard this game is to play," Kaline said before the 1976 opener. "But as a player I also knew when I made a mistake — and they should, too.

"I'm going to try to be objective, without being nasty or critical. I think I can do that. I realize the people are going to be more aware of whatever I say because it's Al Kaline who is saying it. So, I'm going to have to be careful to say exactly what I mean."

Out of the gate, Kaline struggled just as he did as a young ballplayer. Not with his analysis, but with his delivery.

In his 2010 book "Al Kaline: The Biography of a Tigers Icon," former Free Press beat reporter Jim Hawkins wrote:

"Some ex-players are naturals behind the microphone. They just open their mouths and let the witty observations and analysis flow. Al Kaline was not one of those guys. ...

"He felt uncomfortable. He wasn't a polished speaker. He had never received any training in that regard. And, by nature, he was never a glib or talkative guy.

"Kaline certainly knew the game. And he definitely had plenty to say. But he didn't always know the best way to say it.

"As a result, during his first years in the booth, he was often criticized in print and mocked in private for his grammatical errors and fractured syntax during Tigers telecasts.

"The attacks hurt. Al didn't like playing the broadcasting buffoon. So he worked hard to hone his skills and master his performance behind a microphone, just as he had done so many years earlier on the baseball diamond."

Even during that first season, despite his struggles, Kaline had won over Free Press columnist George Puscas. By midseason, Puscas wrote:

"I never would have figured it, but here is the brightest, most refreshing new voice among the sports commentators.

"Through his years as a player, Kaline never was all that outspoken and never particularly critical, not publicly anyway, of his peers. Nor was he all that articulate.

"Now, though, his work as a commentator on Tiger telecasts reveals not only a deep knowledge of the game, which is not surprising, but

a willingness to point out blunders afield."

Hawkins, in his book, wrote that Kell, Kaline's good friend, "helped smooth out some of the remaining rough edges and make Al more comfortable with the spoken word."

Kell wrote about Kaline extensively

CONTINUED ON PAGE 119

Signing off

When the Tigers announced that Al Kaline would leave Channel 50's broadcast team with Frank Beckmann for the front office, Kaline said: "I had the best job in Detroit baseball. I worked 40 games a year." A variety of former Tigers replaced Kaline for the second half of the 2001 season on WKBD-TV. Former catcher Lance Parrish, with Kaline's recommendation, landed the full-time gig for 2002. The Free Press wrote in June 2001 that Kaline the broadcaster should be remembered for ...

☒ All those years with fellow Tigers great George Kell.

☒ How he would provide one too many easy clues and give away Kell's trivia questions.

☒ The occasional name that gave Al problems, like "Tom Seavers."

☒ The occasional cliché that gave him problems, like when he said Tigers players were "frothing at the bit" to get the season started.

☒ How he became an incisive analyst, never hesitant to criticize the Tigers when they needed it — and they need it now.

CONTINUED FROM PAGE 118

in his 1998 autobiography, "Hello Everybody, I'm George Kell." Including:

"When Al first started broadcasting, I think he felt a little insecure. That's natural. He's such as a great player and always performed to such a high level, I think he was wondering if he could meet such high expectations in a new profession. ...

"Because Al knows the game so well, though, he's able to analyze when a player makes a mistake. Al also is quick to point out some little good thing that a player does to help a team that a fan might not even notice."

— Gene Myers

Kaline's third career: A call to the front office

After 22 seasons on the diamond and 26 more in the booth, Al Kaline moved to the Tigers' front office in a stunning move that nearly sent him into retirement once and for all.

With the Tigers already 10 games under .500 and 12½ games out of first place on June 18, 2001, owner Mike Ilitch unveiled his Tigers Baseball Committee, a five-man panel that he hoped would turn around the fortunes of his floundering franchise. At the time, Ilitch's hockey team, the Detroit Red Wings, had reached the playoffs for 11 straight years and had won back-to-back Stanley Cups in 1997-98. Ilitch's baseball team, purchased from Domino's Pizza founder Tom Monaghan in August 1992, hadn't reached the playoffs since 1987 and hadn't posted a winning record since 1993.

"I'd like to run the day-to-day operation of the Tigers the way I run it on the Red Wings," Ilitch said. "We've had hundreds of meetings over the years and a lot of telephone conferences on the Wings. It's led to great chemistry and great success."

For his committee, Ilitch picked the team president, a title he had held since John McHale Jr.'s recent departure for Tampa Bay; Kaline, with the title of assistant to the president; Kaline's teammate Willie Horton, with the title of assistant to baseball operations; Randy Smith, general manager since October 1996; and Phil Garner, manager since October 1999.

Ilitch declared that adding Kaline and Horton to the front office meant "more brainpower, expertise and experience." Ilitch insisted that Kaline leave Channel 50's broadcast booth immediately to avoid what Kaline called "a credibility problem." Among his responsibilities would be scouting the franchise's minor-league talent and looking at potential acqui-

In 2002, Al Kaline showed Dave Dombrowski around Tiger Town on the new boss' first day in Lakeland. "Taking a tour of the facility with Al Kaline — you have to pinch yourself," he said. "I got chills."
JULIAN H. GONZALEZ

sitions.

"If I can help in any little way to get this organization back to how Willie and I remember it," Kaline said, "I'm willing to do it. I think I have a little knowledge about the game, and I think I'll be a little more free to express my opinion."

Asked what his first suggestion might be, Kaline replied with a smile: "Get more pitching."

Kaline, however, quickly became disenchanted with the committee's direction and asked Ilitch for a clarification of his role. Ilitch gave Kaline carte blanche to involve himself as he saw fit.

"I enjoyed spending time with some of the players," Kaline said later, "and they seemed to like the fact that I was there."

By November 2001, after a dismal 66-96 season, Ilitch told Kaline that he was on the verge of hiring Dave Dombrowski from the Florida Marlins as team president. Kaline applauded the move — and suggested Ilitch also eliminate his baseball committee.

A few weeks shy of his 67th birthday, Kaline expressed a desire to continue in some role but also to retire after one more year, which would be his 50th with the Tigers.

"If that doesn't happen, it's not the

most important thing in the world," he said. "Two things I know I won't do: I won't go back to broadcasting because I don't want to do the traveling anymore, and I won't do PR, like making speeches or helping to sell tickets."

Within two months, Dombrowski disbanded the baseball committee but appointed Kaline and Horton as special assistants to the president. "He seems to want my input, which I feel good about," Kaline said. "I'll be working in spring training, helping evaluate the team. I will probably make several trips to our minor-league teams and give the president my thoughts on our minor-league system."

Kaline said he relished the assignment, especially because it did not involve meetings, "it'll be more one-on-one" and "I'll be in uniform a lot more."

He reiterated that he still intended to retire after the 2002 season, but he said that Dombrowski hinted he wanted him to stick around longer.

Dombrowski worked nearly 14 years in Detroit. Kaline outlasted him by another 4½ years, as special assistant to the new general manager, Al Avila. Each spring in Lakeland, Kaline happily donned his No. 6 with the old English D.

— Gene Myers

Fans waited at Metro Airport after Al Kaline's Hall of Fame election. The Free Press landed an executive interview by sending Mick McCabe to New York. He located Kaline's flight to Detroit, purchased a first-class ticket, woke him from a nap and asked his wife to change seats. "Louise wasn't thrilled," McCabe wrote in April 2020, "but Kaline was incredibly gracious and amazingly humble as he spoke about his career and his love for the Tigers and their fans."

CONTINUED FROM PAGE 117
room suite. One for him, one for us and one for Duke Snyder. We tried to go to bed at 11 p.m., but we couldn't sleep."

The BBWAA results were revealed Wednesday morning, and Kaline and Snyder talked with the media in New York. Then Mr. and Mrs. Al Hamilton boarded a flight to Detroit and held another news conference at Tiger Stadium.

Kaline received an interesting call from Tigers owner John Fetzer.

"He sounded more enthusiastic than I was," Kaline said with a laugh. "He was telling me this was the greatest thing that ever happened to me. He sounded like my father. He was very close to me. When the kids were young and we'd fly back from spring training he'd help Louise babysit the kids. He's been good to me."

The Hall of Fame already had several Kaline mementoes, such as the bat and ball from his 3,000th hit. Hall of Fame officials asked Louise Kaline to sort through all the trophies, awards and assorted memorabilia that had accrued in the Kaline household over their 25 years of marriage and decide which should be sent for the Kaline induction exhibit in Cooperstown.

"We never dreamed he would make it on the first ballot," she said.

Louise met Al during their high school days in Baltimore. "I had never even seen him in uniform," she recalled.

The couple dated for three years before marrying when both were 19. "I was always very happy and proud for him," she said. "And I've always felt like I was part of it. I've been with him from the very beginning."

When the "Hamiltons" landed in Detroit, a couple hundred fans had gathered to greet the newest Hall of Famer, who obliged with autographs.

"The fans in Detroit haven't had a great deal to cheer about in the last few years," Kaline said. "Now, in some very small way, maybe the people have something to be proud of. Maybe they can raise their heads up and say, 'Hey, I'm from Detroit.'"

A short time later at The Corner, Kaline said: "I never wished I was playing anywhere else but in Detroit. But there were many times when I wished I was playing for a winning team. ...

"I don't know if I could have survived in New York, Chicago, the big cities. Detroit is a big city, but it's a small town, too."

A Hall of a career

By the numbers

Year	G	PA	AB	R	H	2B	3B	HR	RBI	SB	CS	BB	SO	BA	OBP	SLG	TB	IBB
1953	30	30	28	9	7	0	0	1	2	1	0	1	5	.250	.300	.357	10	0
1954	138	535	504	43	139	18	3	4	43	9	5	22	45	.276	.305	.347	175	2
1955	152	681	588	121	200	24	8	27	102	6	8	82	57	.340	.421	.546	321	12
1956	153	693	617	96	194	32	10	27	128	7	1	70	55	.314	.383	.530	327	4
1957	149	636	577	83	170	29	4	23	90	11	9	43	38	.295	.343	.478	276	7
1958	146	607	543	84	170	34	7	16	85	7	4	54	47	.313	.374	.490	266	6
1959	136	594	511	85	167	19	2	27	94	10	4	72	42	.327	.410	.530	271	12
1960	147	629	551	77	153	29	4	15	68	19	4	65	47	.278	.354	.426	235	3
1961	153	665	586	116	190	41	7	19	82	14	1	66	42	.324	.393	.515	302	2
1962	100	452	398	78	121	16	6	29	94	4	0	47	39	.304	.376	.593	236	3
1963	145	616	551	89	172	24	3	27	101	6	4	54	48	.312	.375	.514	283	12
1964	146	608	525	77	154	31	5	17	68	4	1	75	51	.293	.383	.469	246	6
1965	125	474	399	72	112	18	2	18	72	6	0	72	49	.281	.388	.471	188	11
1966	142	572	479	85	138	29	1	29	88	5	5	81	66	.288	.392	.534	256	7
1967	131	550	458	94	141	28	2	25	78	8	2	83	47	.308	.411	.541	248	10
1968	102	389	327	49	94	14	1	10	52	6	4	55	39	.287	.392	.428	140	7
1969	131	518	456	74	124	17	0	21	69	1	2	54	61	.272	.346	.447	204	4
1970	131	555	467	64	130	24	4	16	71	2	2	77	49	.278	.377	.450	210	5
1971	133	501	405	69	119	19	2	15	54	4	6	82	57	.294	.416	.462	187	9
1972	106	314	278	46	87	11	2	10	32	1	0	28	33	.313	.374	.475	132	5
1973	91	347	310	40	79	13	0	10	45	4	1	29	28	.255	.320	.394	122	4
1974	147	630	558	71	146	28	2	13	64	2	2	65	75	.262	.337	.389	217	2
TOTAL	**2,834**	**11,596**	**10,116**	**1,622**	**3,007**	**498**	**75**	**399**	**1,582**	**137**	**65**	**1,277**	**1,020**	**.297**	**.376**	**.480**	**4,852**	**133**

ALBERT WILLIAM KALINE
DETROIT A.L., 1953 - 1974
TWELFTH PLAYER TO REACH ELITE 3,000-HIT
PLATEAU. SOCKED 399 HOMERS AND ATTAINED
.297 CAREER AVERAGE, WITH NINE YEARS IN
.300 CLASS. FINISHED IN ALL-TIME TOP 15
WITH 2,834 GAMES, 3,007 HITS, 1,583 RUNS
BATTED IN AND 4,852 TOTAL BASES. PLAYED
100 OR MORE GAMES 20 YEARS AND HAD 242
CONSECUTIVE ERRORLESS GAMES IN OUTFIELD,
1970-1972, FOR A.L. RECORDS. LED IN HITS
AND WON BATTING TITLE IN 1955 AT AGE 20.

A league

RBIs

Al Kaline never led the American League in RBIs, though he finished second twice. The races:

1956

1. Mickey Mantle, NYY	130
2. Al Kaline, DET	128
3. Vic Wertz, CLE	106

1963

1. Dick Stuart, BOS	118
2. Al Kaline, DET	101
3. Harmon Killebrew, MIN	96

Al Kaline used his picture-perfect swing to go from the sandlots of Baltimore to the old ballpark in Detroit to the hallowed halls of Cooperstown.
MALCOLM EMMONS

DETROIT FREE PRESS

Mickey Mantle cleared the rightfield roof three times in Detroit.

apart

How Mr. Tiger compared to the AL's league leaders over the years

DETROIT FREE PRESS

During the 15 seasons Al Kaline and Norm Cash were teammates in Detroit — from 1960-74 — they combined for 647 homers. Cash hit 373; Kaline hit 274.

Batting

Al Kaline won the AL batting title at age 20 in 1955, then finished in the top three five more times over the next 12 seasons. The races:

1955	
1. Al Kaline, DET	.340
2. Vic Power, KCA	.319
3. George Kell, CHW	.312

1959	
1. Harvey Kuenn, DET	.353
2. Al Kaline, DET	.327
3. Pete Runnels, BOS	.314

1961	
1. Norm Cash, DET	.361
2. Al Kaline, DET	.324
3. Jim Piersall, CLE	.322

1963	
1. Carl Yastrzemski, BOS	.321
2. Al Kaline, DET	.312
3. Rich Rollins, MIN	.307

1966	
1. Frank Robinson, BAL	.316
2. Tony Oliva, MIN	.307
3. Al Kaline, DET	.288

1967	
1. Carl Yastrzemski, BOS	.326
2. Frank Robinson, BAL	311
3. Al Kaline, DET	.308

MVP

Al Kaline never won the AL MVP vote, though he finished in the top three in voting three times:

1955

Kaline, at just 20, led the AL in hits (200), batting average (.340) and total bases (321), and added 27 home runs and 102 RBIs. He finished second, however, behind Yankees catcher Yogi Berra, who matched Kaline's homer total but hit just .272. The vote was close, 218 points to 201.

1956

Kaline dropped off a bit at 21, as his average dropped to .314. He hit 27 homers again, though, and had 108 RBIs. This time, he finished a distant third in the voting (142), behind the Yankees' Berra (186) and Mickey Mantle (336), who won unanimously following a Triple Crown — .353 average, 52 homers, 130 RBIs.

1963

Another 27-homer season, along with a .312 average and 101 RBIs, landed Kaline second in the balloting again, 248-148, this time behind a new Yankees catcher, Elston Howard, who had a .287 average, 28 homers and 85 RBIs. If opposing managers had a vote, however, the outcome might have been different — Kaline led the AL with 12 intentional walks.

– Ryan Ford

Face of the

A l Kaline is among the top five in virtually every major offensive category in Tigers history, from games to WAR (Wins Above Replacement) to intentional walks. Where he stands in 11 key stats:

Games

Al Kaline	2,834
Ty Cobb	2,806
Lou Whitaker	2,390
Charlie Gehringer	2,323
Alan Trammell	2,293

Hits

Ty Cobb	3,900
Al Kaline	3,007
Charlie Gehringer	2,839
Harry Heilmann	2,499
Sam Crawford	2,466

RBIs

Ty Cobb	1,811
Al Kaline	1,582
Harry Heilmann	1,446
Charlie Gehringer	1,427
Sam Crawford	1,262

Total bases

Ty Cobb	5,466
Al Kaline	4,852
Charlie Gehringer	4,257
Harry Heilmann	3,778
Lou Whitaker	3,651

Doubles

Ty Cobb	665
Charlie Gehringer	574
Al Kaline	498
Harry Heilmann	497
Lou Whitaker	420

franchise

Home runs

Al Kaline	399
Norm Cash	373
Miguel Cabrera	339
Hank Greenberg	306
Willie Horton	262

WAR

Player	WAR
Ty Cobb	144.7
Al Kaline	92.8
Charlie Gehringer	83.8
Lou Whitaker	75.1
Alan Trammell	70.7

Runs

Player	Runs
Ty Cobb	2,087
Charlie Gehringer	1,775
Al Kaline	1,622
Lou Whitaker	1,386
Donnie Bush	1,243

At-bats

Player	At-bats
Ty Cobb	10,597
Al Kaline	10,116
Charlie Gehringer	8,860
Lou Whitaker	8,570
Alan Trammell	8,288

Walks

Player	Walks
Al Kaline	1,277
Lou Whitaker	1,197
Charlie Gehringer	1,186
Ty Cobb	1,148
Donnie Bush	1,125

Intentional walks

Player	IW
Miguel Cabrera	164
Al Kaline	133
Norm Cash	109
Lou Whitaker	79
Willie Horton	78

"I don't like the word 'superstar.' I think I was a quality player. Not as good as a few, but better than most."

– Al Kaline

Since Comerica Park's opening in April 2000, Al Kaline's statue stood poised to snare a long drive beyond the seats in left-center.
MANDI WRIGHT